JOY, DESPAIR, AND HOPE

Joy, Despair, and Hope

Reading Psalms

EDWARD FELD

CASCADE *Books* • Eugene, Oregon

JOY, DESPAIR, AND HOPE
Reading Psalms

Cascade Books
An Imprint of Wipf and Stock Publishers
199 W. 8th Ave., Suite 3
Eugene, OR 97401

www.wipfandstock.com

ISBN 13: 978-1-4982-1532-9

Cataloging-in-Publication data:

Feld, Edward, 1943–

Joy, despair, and hope : reading Psalms / Edward Feld.

xiv + 154 p.; 23 cm—Includes bibliographical references and index.

ISBN 13: 978-1-4982-1532-9

1. Bible—O.T.—Psalms—Criticism, interpretation, etc. I. Title.

BS1433 F45 2013

Manufactured in the USA

To my children,
Lisa and Uri,
May this work accompany you on your journey

*"Behold I come
with a book written about me."*

PSALM 40:8

Contents

Preface

THERE ARE SOME MOMENTS that just stick with you. They are the pegs on which we hang insights that have accompanied us as we construct our lives. When I was in college, a speaker quoted the line from Psalms, "From the depths I call to You . . ." The point he was making was that the Bible, and in turn later Jewish texts, deal with the most profound human emotions. In late teenage, full of the *Sturm und Drang* of the moment of self-discovery and self-definition, I knew those depths out of which I called, they were the depths of aloneness and fear that everyone may feel but which adolescents, taking their first steps into independent adult life, feel intensely. Hearing this phrase, it felt as though a voice from the biblical age echoed my own inner life.

The immediate reaction may have been that of a kid suffering through late adolescence, nevertheless, the memory has continued to be profoundly significant in my development as an adult. In college I felt that here was a text, the Psalms, that had the possibility of speaking to me in a way that I missed in the philosophy courses I attended and since then I have come to feel that I needed religious poetry to accompany me on my journey, and that in those times when I opened up the book of Psalms I might find verses with which my inner life could resonate. A poet who lived twenty-five hundred years ago could speak the truth of my own soul.

Though the line from Psalms that I quoted has continued to accompany me in adulthood, when I would read the remainder of the psalm, I thought its poetry less inviting. The psalm as a whole was more problematic for me; it raised issues and themes that were theologically troubling. I had to work at dissecting the psalm, questioning it, debating it, before I felt that its totality might hold some power for me.

Psalm 130
A song of ascents:
From the depths I call to You, God;
Adonai, hear my voice.
Let Your ears listen closely
to the sound of my plea.
If You continue recalling sin,
who can survive, Adonai?
But with You forgiveness is found—
for which we are in awe.
I have waited for God,
my whole being waited,
hoping for a word from God.
My whole being waits for God,
more than the morning watchmen watch for the dawn.
Look to God, Israel,
for God is full of compassion;
generously, God redeems.
Surely God will redeem Israel from all its sins.

I know the depth out of which I call. There are moments when I find little meaning in what I am doing, times when all activity seems futile. When I think of sin, I contemplate the missed opportunities of my life—the challenges life has offered to which I haven't risen; the courage that I lacked. More, I know the people I've failed to help, the responsibilities I've failed to meet, the time I've wasted, the petty thieveries I've committed—psychologically and physically. I would like what I have achieved to wipe away the failures. I'd like to be considered good, successful in having redeemed the possibilities of my soul.

But so much of the time I don't really believe that is possible. The forgiving God is not close at hand to me. I know the judgmental universe but not the forgiving one. Yes, there are days that I forgive myself for being merely human, imperfect, conflicted, wanting to do good, wanting to rise to my responsibilities, and wanting to throw off restraint. But the guilt—the knowledge of my recurring lassitude—returns a day later.

And yet I hope and pray for the possibility of starting fresh—of entering the universe with joy, with a sense of fullness and love. Each day I rise and look forward to a way to redemption. How might I be happy with who I am? How might I find the field for the full expression of my soul?

The biblical poet seems to go back and forth too. In one verse there is an expression of faith—an understanding that the compassionate God will always forgive those who approach God faithfully. For this the poet is truly in awe. Yet, we also are led to understand that the poet has not yet actually felt that forgiving presence. The supplicant awaits word from God. The manifold repetition of waiting for God expresses something different from the assurance of God's forgiveness enunciated in the earlier verse. The poem somehow seems to hold onto the contradictoriness of life.

It is the knowledge that even the biblical poet waits—longs for and hopes—that allows my sense of God's absence to have religious legitimacy, allows it to stand alongside that poet's expression. The poet, though, has more self-assurance than I that the redeeming moment, the ultimate forgiveness, will come shortly. The poet's image of waiting is that of the watchman waiting for the dawn. The dawn always comes; the watchman knows that it will come sometime soon; the job of the watchman is to search the sky for the first light that greets each new day approximately at this hour —the only question is one of minutes. But for me, the question is more fundamental: the question is whether it will ever occur.

Interestingly, the note of reassurance on which the poem ends is not personal. The promise of God's presence and compassion evoked is a promise given to the collectivity of Israel. Rather than the individual praying to God, Israel as a collective whole is now addressed. And in the end, the poet has moved from first-person calling to third-person address. One might wonder if this line is even the prayer of the supplicant or the response of the priest to a supplicant's earlier prayerful lament.

Perhaps the poet ends with an understanding that the individual might never receive an answer from God, but that the supplicant is addressed through a tradition. In this reading, the comfort we have arises from the texts and rituals of the tradition not from a personal response from God. The poet only overcomes the sense of absence by asking us to lose ourselves in collective memory and in attaching ourselves to communal promise. Perhaps I can find solace in the thought that the biblical poet, too, had to give up the idea of hearing God's voice, of experiencing God's presence.

Is that really a sufficient answer? This book is a struggle with that question. It explores the voices in psalms in an attempt to see how these authors dealt with and responded to the presence and absence of God, the contemplation of human finitude, loneliness, and fear and the possibilities of joy and redemption. These were the first people who wrestled with religious faith; perhaps their articulations will give direction to my own journey. Reading them, I might find echoes of my own struggles, and hope for some resolution.

Acknowledgments

My first teacher of Psalms, Professor Nahum Sarna, taught me how to read these poems slowly and carefully and so had a decisive effect on the way I read all biblical literature. His memory is a blessing, and his influence can be seen throughout this work. I first began teaching Psalms as the Rabbi of the Society for Advancement of Judaism where I incorporated their study into the Saturday morning service. It was in that context and among that special congregation that I discovered that I had something to say about these poems and that it was important for people to hear their message.

Several readers have helped in the preparation of this manuscript. My friend, the writer John Clayton, encouraged their publication. Professor Steven Geller of the Jewish Theological Seminary was most generous in giving of his time to review the manuscript for any scholarly mistakes. My wife, Merle, an exquisite editor, read the manuscript several times and offered important editorial comment. Her constant encouragement of my work was critical in my being able to see this book to publication. Equally, it was a delight to be able to share this book with my daughter, Lisa, herself an editor, and be able to incorporate her editorial comments throughout.

Introduction

THROUGH THE AGES, PSALMS have been read to uplift the soul, to comfort the sick, to console those who mourn, to celebrate moments of blessing experienced by individuals and the community, to instruct the faithful and the doubter in the ways of the Divine, and to provide the words which express the state of our souls—the words of prayer. Yet I sense that the book of Psalms, which until recently was the book of the Bible most widely known, most constantly read, and most expressive of the inner lives of generations of Christians and Jews, is a closed one for our generation. The language of Psalms seems alien to us, its purposes hidden, its poetics foreign.

The intention of this work is to try to recapture some of the psalms of the book of Psalms for modern readers, to look closely at them and to show how they can speak to us yet again. This book represents my own journey through these psalms, my own spiritual search, and my hope is that in describing my own relation to particular psalms other readers will be able to find their voices within these texts, too.

The Psalms are not a literary unity emanating from a single author or a concise moment in history. Rather, even by its own admission, the book is an agglomeration from a variety of sources. Psalms speak with many voices, describe many moods, incorporate many different styles.

To be sure, the great bulk of psalms—almost half the book—bear the name of David, which is why, traditionally, he has been thought of as the author of the entire book. Already in biblical times this attribution was understood literally, and so some of the psalms are ascribed to particular moments in David's life; for instance, Psalm 3 is said to be written, "As he ran away from Absalom, his son," and Psalm 51, "When Nathan the prophet came to him after his having come into Bathsheba." Some medieval commentators thought they could find hints of David's life in each of the psalms. The *I* of Psalms became the story of David's inner life.

1

Yet the Hebrew preposition, the letter *lamed,* which precedes these names, covers a variety of meanings. While *lamed* may be the preposition indicating authorship, equivalent to the English "by," as some have traditionally understood it, it can also mean "dedicated to," or "in the manner of." Moreover, the name *David* may not be personal but might refer to the entire dynasty—the Davidic kingdom, and therefore his name may simply indicate that the poem comes from the royal, that is Davidic, library—the preposition *lamed* meaning here "belonging to."

Certainly many psalms were written hundreds of years after David's reign (between approximately 970 and 930 BCE). Psalm 137, which speaks of the Babylonian exile and asks, "How can we sing the praise of God in a foreign land?" was clearly written some four hundred years after David died, when the Davidic kingdom had come to an end and Jews sat on foreign soil. In fact, in the early part of the twentieth century, it was fashionable to attribute most psalms to the exile and after—to the Second Temple period. However, by midcentury, when modern archaeology uncovered a long Middle Eastern poetic tradition, scholars realized that many psalms deserved earlier dating. Today most scholars would agree that the psalmic tradition spans hundreds of years, from perhaps the beginning of the Hebrew kingdom in the tenth century or soon after, through the Judean exile in 587 BCE, and into the time of the return—almost sixty years later—and into the Second Temple period that followed.

In all, some ten different historical figures or families are listed as authors of psalms in inscriptions in the book itself, including Moses and Solomon, and less-known figures like Heman and Ethan the Ezrahite (Psalms 88 and 89 respectively are ascribed to them), who are mentioned in 1 Kings 5:11 as wise men.

Psalms thus display the styles of multiple authors, the changing fashions of centuries of literary production, as well as a variety of settings and a range of moods. Some psalms are national or royal and contain a recitation of the great moments of Israelite history or a plea for the defense of the country or prayer for the king's victory or for victory in battle; some psalms are songs of thanksgiving—for the daily miracles of life, the abundance of gifts nature brings, and the order of the universe; many of these psalms may easily be associated with temple sacrifices. But what is surprising about the Psalms, and what has given the book its special appeal through the centuries, is that other unexpected voices are heard as well: descriptions of despair, expressions of pain, songs of longing for a God whose presence can no longer be felt. Psalmists tell stories of hurt, of illness, of loss of faith along with personal expressions of deliverance.

Fully more than half the psalms use the first-person singular *I*. Peter Berger, the sociologist of religion, once remarked that in Psalms we encounter the first moment in which Western literature gives expression to the individual self. When we read ancient literature, we are used to meeting the *I* of kings and heroes, figures found in epic poetry, but in the psalms we also meet the pleas of the ordinary, lonely person who is presented as the stranger in the land; we hear the voice of the disinherited, the lowliest, the abject, as well as that of the king. Here is the fulfillment of the promise of Genesis that all people are created in the image of God, for it is to the plea of the lowly that God will respond, a claim which the psalmist puts in God's own voice (Psalm 12:6: "From the dispoilation of the poor, and the prayer of the lowly, I will rise up . . ."). These are the prayers not only of kings, of the elite, but of everyman, everywoman.

It is the introspective voice of the self which particularly comes to the fore in Psalms, and which makes the book especially appealing. These psalms express the cry of the heart and its opposite—the joy of experiencing God's presence. A psalmic author can in one moment describe a sense of abandonment: "My God, my God, why have you deserted me?" and in the next moment incomparable wonder and thanksgiving as when an author imagines being led by a caring sheepherder to placid waters, "Your staff and Your rod will comfort me," and then joining in a meal at God's own table. In fact, the discerning editor of the book of Psalms has placed these two opposite expressions side by side—in Psalms 22 and 23. The book consciously depicts a range of human emotions.

While some of these poems, like songs of thanksgiving, seem appropriate in a temple setting, others, especially those that express a loss of faith and describe hurt at feeling God's abandonment, seem inappropriate for recitation in the temple. Interestingly, while many of the psalmic ascriptions are to Levitical clans associated with temple worship, the larger number of ascriptions are Davidic (i.e., attributed to a nonpriestly authority). We ought not to make too much of this distinction since it was David's son Solomon who built the temple and dedicated it, and it was David himself who accompanied the ark with song and dance to Jerusalem. Still, the ascription to David may point to an extra-temple tradition of religious song, and clearly those who attached these songs to moments of David's life saw them as being composed and recited outside the temple (some, for instance, are ascribed to moments of his personal exile). Several psalms specifically confirm this sense that the setting of psalms is outside the temple. For instance, when the poet of Psalm 63 writes of thirsting to see God as he or she once did in the temple, the author is clearly not writing in a temple setting but is situated at some distance from the temple.

To be sure, there may have been a tradition of Levitical singing in the temple, but there were other settings for songs as well. I like to think of one such setting as that of pilgrims coming up to Jerusalem, sitting around the campfire on the road or at the southern mountaintop approaching the city. In the latter setting, to one side stretched the desert and the Valley of Hinnom, on the other were the peaks of the Judean hills. Resting on the hillside, the pilgrims could peer down at the temple perched atop a small hill in the valley below. They could see inside the temple precincts, smoke emanating from the fire on the altar. Altogether the view here may have been more encompassing than that available to the worshiper in the temple itself. So here, around the campfire, leaders sang songs. Poets, elders, men of wisdom, prophetic women, could voice their own compositions. Some Levites may have come up from the city below, joining the pilgrims around their fires, leading songs that initiated the pilgrims into the ritual they would participate in the following morning. These Levites might especially emphasize the need for purity and a life of righteousness as a requirement for the efficacy of the offering on the morrow, that the pilgrims might properly enter the temple and have their prayers answered. Travelers may have responded by describing the hurts that had brought them to seek answers at the temple. Thus, a tradition of extra-temple singing was born, so that in a later time, in exile, one poet can say that people requested him to sing as he had in the old days, but he had to hang up his harp, because the setting for those songs was always the pilgrimage and now there was nothing to look towards (Psalm 137).

Whatever their origins, these poems touch on themes that captivate us even when we cannot uncover their original context. The songs capture varying moods, they talk of joy, of blessing, of the goodness to be experienced in the world. Others talk of the loss of faith, of life as troubled, of God as seemingly absent. Almost all of these psalms seek some resolution: the loss of faith is turned into a moment of prayer, attempts are made to restore hope, or new answers to the persistent questions of life are offered. It is the progress of these ideas which this book examines, for these psalmists as they explore a range of human situations, a breadth of human feeling, develop a language of prayer which may allow us to give voice to our own emotions, and may offer us a language of faithfulness which does not compromise our own ambivalence, our own questioning of the tradition.

I have approached the psalms as displaying poetic art—thus, they should be read as whole poems, not simply as particularly suggestive individual lines. I have treated each psalm as a unified literary unit and tried to uncover the journey the poet engages in. I examine each poem in itself: I have not used a comparative approach, nor have I attempted to group psalms in particular genres or contexts.

Along with explicating some of the concerns of the psalmist, I also try to describe the building blocks of psalmic art: how did the biblical poet conceive of a line, a stanza? What is the glue that holds a poem together? What is the relation of beginnings and endings? Along with understanding some of the theological claims of several psalms, these concerns dominate the discussion of the first several chapters of the book. Understanding the literary nature of psalms helps us uncover their meaning. But even as I do this, I have dealt only with whole poems and have not quoted here and there in the Bible, as most critical authors do: each chapter presents a different psalm for understanding and consideration. I want readers to meet the biblical text whole, not through a filter.

I want to encourage readers to look at psalms with fresh eyes and to view them personally. I have not encumbered the text with scholarly philological discussion, nor with overly footnoted debates, for I want to address an interested laity and not a specialized elite, though I hope the latter as well as the former finds this work instructive.

I take seriously the religious outlook of psalms. If these poems are to speak to us, they ought to be able to convey a message that makes sense in our world. As we leave each psalm we ought to ask: What did the biblical poet try to convey? How does it correlate with our own experience? Instead of being distant, psalms should be the biblical text closest to us, for these poems offer a personal, individual glimpse of the inner soul of biblical Israel as almost no other book of the Bible does.

This book is composed of three sections. First, I describe what we might consider the norm of a biblical outlook. Since the questioning of God has theological assumptions, it seems appropriate to place at the fore those psalms which express the regnant theology of which other psalmists despair. These are psalms that have confidence in a sense of order, an ultimately just world, the good life and its rewards. We have all had such days when we wake up and feel the world is ready for us.

5

Then I look to the psalms where the author has lost faith in this world. These authors may be describing illness or defeat or the injustice and lies that seem to permeate society. Like Job, most of these psalmists do not see the fault as lying in their own behavior; rather they experience themselves as meeting an irrational universe. Many of these writers no longer see the world as coherent. Their despair is expressed in graphic terms, and they offer a public voice for our darkest moments.

Finally, I look to those psalms that explore a new theology, that find reason to turn to God even when the feeling of absence is overwhelming. The ability to find hope even when simple faith has been shattered is the especial gift of psalms.

A word must be added about those psalms not covered in this book. I have not included psalms that are simple poetic recitals of Israelite history—these psalms are almost self-explanatory. Nor have I included royal psalms—kings praying for victory in battle, for defense of the land, or thanking God for delivery in times of siege or war. Nor, for the most part, have I stressed those psalms that are hymns of praise, acknowledgments of the divine presence in all things good. Many of these psalms are enchanting and inspiring and have become liturgical favorites, it is not startling that they are included in the book of Psalms. Their place there is obvious.

But it is the ability to express something more, the personal moments of doubt and despair alongside the acknowledgment of blessing, which makes the book of Psalms so precious. As I have remarked, psalms capture the various moods of life and reading them we bridge time, for we can hear the individual voices of people living in ancient Israel. When we listen with that ear, we can also hear the voices of generations of Jews and Christians, who, sounding these words, found expression of their own inner lives. In these psalms, we find responses to the pummeling of life and the power of these poems lies in the degree to which they can resonate with our own spirit, the inner prompting of our own hearts. These psalms offer the first and clearest expression of the pathos of human existence. And it is this aspect that my work explores.

Thankfully, the recent trend in biblical scholarship is to try to respect and understand the Bible in its literary wholeness—an approach that has been especially fruitful. Applying these methods to psalms, scholars such as Gunkel, Westermann, and recently Bruegemann have provided tools for understanding the literary frameworks for psalms by talking of types of psalms and seeing how individual authors develop biblical themes. It is Brueggeman's threefold division of psalms into orientation, disorientation, and hope that inspired the tripartite division of this book, though this book differs markedly from his formulation.

A word as to translation. In arriving at my own translation I have consulted a variety of previous translations from the enduring King James Version to the New Jewish Publication Society Translation; the latter has been especially important for the version readers will encounter here. In addition, *The Psalms* translated by Peter Levi (1976) has been a special inspiration for many of my renderings. But I have departed from all of these, sometimes with slight changes, sometimes with significant variation for a variety of reasons. First, I try to be more consistent in my translation of the Hebrew than is true of any of these versions, so that readers can sense the flow of the Hebrew. Second, I wanted the English to be clear to modern readers. Third, in my rendition, I tried to convey some sense of the poetic art that I then comment on. Every translation has to penetrate the distance between ancient Hebrew and modern consciousness and come to a decision about what the Hebrew means and, of course, some of the decisions of translation I have made differ with the way other versions might understand a phrase or even the entire poem. (I should add that by the time of publication, I have revised the translation many times and find it impossible to see anymore whether I derived a phrase from one source or another.)

A particular challenge of translation involves the issue of how to translate the personal name of God. The Hebrew reader does not even pronounce the letters of God's name but instead whenever they occur uses a substitution: *Adonai*, "my Lord." Thus, from the very beginning, the King James Version translated the Hebrew word *Elohim*—the more generic name for God—as "God" and the personal name of God as "Lord." I don't feel that the English *Lord* is evocative any longer and have therefore chosen to use the Hebrew *Adonai* in English, attempting to signal that it is a personal name for God. I realize that no solution to this problem of translation is adequate.[1]

Psalms are poetry, exhibiting all the characteristics we have come to recognize in poetic arts: use of metaphor, subtle ambiguity, conciseness of language, elevated language, and even the testing of the boundaries of language and the creation of new verbal forms. It is precisely these poetic arts that frequently create the greatest conundrum in understanding the meaning of any poem, more so in the case of the Bible, which is so distant

---

1. In Exodus, God's personal name is explained as, "Tell them that I am has sent you."

from us in linguistic usage and cultural context. And because psalms are art, there is an ultimate moment in which the scholarly study of the text reaches its limits and critical listening becomes decisive in establishing meaning. Yet, it is a close reading and attentive listening, along with our own sense of empathy that can allow us to enter the poem in its fullness. Frequently, it is before this point that academic scholarship stops. That was the case with my own education: my teachers were brilliant scholars able to analyze the range of meanings of each word but, after looking at each element in the poem, few of them ever put the text back together so that the unitary voice of the single psalm could once again speak to us. It is not only a matter of taking that last step, as if this were merely the icing on the cake. Rather, in a poem, if we do not comprehend the whole, we may not properly understand the individual words and lines. I am grateful to my teachers who taught me how to be attentive to each word in psalms, and I hope that they will appreciate my own contribution in understanding these poems as a whole.

This book is a personal reading of psalms. I try to help readers into psalms by showing the ones I particularly love and respond to. Roughly one-tenth of the entire book of Psalms is represented here. Many readers will want to go on and explore other psalms, finding particular ones with which they fall in love.

I believe that it is not necessarily those psalms which have entered the liturgy, or the ones most frequently quoted, which can speak to our age, rather the personal psalms, the ones in which the self of the author is plumbed, can be most consonant with the language our own souls wish to speak, and it is to them that I have primarily, though not exclusively, turned my attention. My wish is that you, the reader, will come to see in the book of Psalms a place where the soul manifests itself, where nourishment for your own spiritual life can be found. It may be that for a moment you will be able to hear the heart's cry of people who lived thousands of years ago and find their words expressing concerns close to your own heart. When this happens, you will feel what generations have felt as they have found consolation in this book: the surprise that in giving voice to his or her own self, the biblical author expressed something that captures our own finite, painful, and glorious human condition. I hope that my work will help in returning the book of Psalms to contemporary readers.

PART 1

Joy

1

Psalm 1

Beginning

WE BEGIN AT THE beginning—Psalm 1. There is clear intentionality in the final editing of the book of Psalms and in the placement of this psalm at the very beginning. Psalm 1 opens with the words, "Blessed is the person . . ." and the last line of Psalm 150, the last psalm of the book of Psalms, reads, "May everything that has breath praise God." Thus the arc of the book stretches from a single person walking with God to a vision of all creation celebrating God. Equally, the very first word of this psalm, *Ashrei* "blessed" (and in some other translations, "happy") is a fitting invitation for readers as is *hallelujah* ("praise God"), a proper ending.

There were other reasons as well for placing Psalm 1 at the beginning of this book. It conveys a common, we might say normative, theme of biblical theology: good people will receive blessing; evil will be destroyed; there is a just order to the universe that is guaranteed by God. This theology did not go unquestioned in the Bible—Job, for one, in his suffering, finds this point of view to be most problematic, saying in effect, "I suffer, but it is not commensurate with any sins I may have committed." And even many psalms, some of which we shall analyze in later chapters, question the validity of this theology finding it challenged by personal experience. But first the idea needs to be stated before it can be questioned:

PSALM 1

1   Blessed[1] is the person who has not pursued the counsel of the wicked,
    nor stood with sinners on their way
    nor sat with the indolent.

2   Rather, his[2] desire is for the teaching of Adonai,
    intoning his teaching day and night.

3   For he will be as a tree planted astride streams
    bearing fruit in season,
    its leaves never shriveling—
    everything thriving.

4   Not so the wicked,
    who are only like chaff, tossed by the wind.

5   So, the wicked will not stand up in court
    nor sinners in the assembly of the righteous,

6   for Adonai knows the way of the just,
    but the way of the wicked will be lost.

The poem is well ordered and direct. There are constant pairings of good and evil. Every statement about good or evil has its immediate counter in its opposite. There are three such pairs, and we progress from an opening delineation of good and evil through an interesting set of metaphors to a final judgment. The poem is tight, well ordered and explicit in its message—the essential opposition of good and evil and the inevitable outcome of each path.

The theology of the psalm is simple enough, but though the fundamental theological conception behind the poem is simple (good will be rewarded and evil will be punished), the work achieves its power through its literary art; the simple message is clothed with all the talent of psalmic craft. There is use of metaphor; in fact we will see that the turn to metaphor in verses 3 and 4 is pivotal in the development of the central ideas

1. Right off the bat, there is a difficulty in translation. The Hebrew word *ashrei*, the first word of this psalm, has been variously translated as happy, joyous, or fruitful. None of these English words capture the sense of the Hebrew. Although Hebrew has another word for 'blessed', I believe that here blessed comes closest to the meaning of the Hebrew.

2. I am frustrated that I cannot translate this psalm in gender neutral language without sacrificing too many other important considerations. I would like the reader to have as close a sense of the Hebrew as I can transmit and so I want word changes in English to reflect the Hebrew as closely as possible.

of the poem. There are some rhythmic elements, obvious in the Hebrew and not entirely lost in translation—though the rhythm is not constant but changes from verse to verse. But more than the rhythm of the single line is the rhythm of the whole: the continual use of contrast forming a threefold comparison between good and evil that serves to develop a divergent vision as we travel through time.

The basic building blocks of the poem are another biblical poetic device: the use of parallelism, the constant doubling (sometimes tripling) of each thought. A simple theological notion is given depth of meaning through this rhetorical device, and we are invited to enter a world of faithfulness that theology itself could only hint at, but that poetry provides with a concreteness we can touch.

I first studied this poem with a wonderful scholar of the Bible, the late Nahum Sarna. I can never forget his unlocking the sequential development of the first sentence. We are greeted with a set of differing images of evil—ranging from the most culpable to those who are guilty because of the attitudes they foster on the sidelines. First, the poet names the obvious, the "wicked," active participants in underhanded schemes, people who join in a cabal, consciously plotting wrongful activities. Second are the "sinners," those who have missed the mark—not the unrepentant evildoer the first phrase suggests, but the everyday flirter with fudging, the people who convince themselves that this act, which breaks the rules, is not so wrong after all, justifying the deed to themselves by saying that everyone does these things, or by thinking of these acts as small and excusable peccadilloes. And lastly, the "indolent," the slothful, the verbal sideswipers, the ones who sit on the sidelines and scornfully poke fun at everyone else. These last don't perform any action at all, they are the ones who lazily pass the time sitting in cafes engaged in cynical conversation—their joking creates the conditions of an apathetic society able to suffer corruption, it is their rhetoric, their cynical conversational posture that undercuts the good.

Each of these types is not only delineated by a different noun but by a different verb conveying a different degree of involvement and culpability. The first group includes those who "pursue" the counsel of evil—those who walk the walk—those who enthusiastically join in planning and plotting criminal activity. Then, instead of the active verb we first meet, the second group is said to "stand" with sinners. The people who "stand" on the sidelines, the ones who simply enjoy the company of shady types: there may be a romantic thrill in associating with the underworld—these are people not likely to be considered among the sinister elements of society, they may never outrightly commit a crime, perhaps it's just that they like others to know that they have friends who are criminals and enjoy the fact that some notoriety rubs off on them, perhaps they like to be close to those who can act on the urges of which they can only dream: they want some of the thrill to rub off on them. But ultimately, this cheering squad—inevitably, at times their transgressions are more than verbal—helps create the social milieu in which nefarious activity is glorified. And last of all, there are those who like to "sit" around, second-guess everyone, and enjoy their ironic view of the vulnerabilities of those who are "out there" trying to do good. It's an activity that at first glance may seem harmless enough—they just 'sit' and it's just talk, after all . . . These last don't really see themselves as part of any disreputable gang, but because their lives have no purpose, because they are not actively working to establish that which is good, but rather spend their time playing cards, drinking, shooting the breeze, poking fun at "do-gooders," they have helped to create a world in which evil can dominate. And it is not only their indolence and apathy that creates the conditions in which the good person feels isolated but most especially their cynicism.

In this first sentence, the author has not only expressed theological axioms, but poetically created a context of believability, a tangible concrete reality that we can enter into and hold on to. And not incidentally, he has widened the circle of culpability so that even the seemingly innocent may be caught in a web of guilt and responsibility.

What has happened in this parallel arrangement is that the less active have been implicated with the conscious criminal: the indolent have been implicated with the evildoers. Had the poet merely expressed that thought in simple prose, as I have, he might not have convinced us; it all would have sounded too "sermonic." The unfolding poetic parallelism, elaborating just enough, yet articulated with conciseness, forms a tightly wrought argument in which suddenly we realize that we, ourselves, may be implicated, though we never saw the punch coming. In this case, poetry throws a more entangling and convincing net than prose ever could.

Now the poet is ready to offer us, as contrast, the life of the righteous. Interestingly, the verbs used in this new image no longer deal with outer movement—walking, standing, sitting—but the inner life—desiring, thinking. Evil concentrates on outer domination, good on the life of the heart and mind. This may reflect an understanding that the place where a person first finds God is the inner life. It also may be the case that the assertion reflects an observation about the poet's contemporary social reality: the outside world is dominated by power, corruption, and injustice; the faithful have only one realm in which to find God—the private life of the heart.

> Rather, his desire is for the teaching of Adonai,
> intoning his teaching day and night.

This second sentence moves from the threefold structure we initially encountered in the poem to a twofold one, perhaps an indication of the greater unity of purpose of the righteous. The inner life is made up of mind and heart, speech and thought, and both are involved in the same activity: the study and appreciation of God's teaching. The sense of unified existence is concretely emphasized by the poet's insistence that the righteous engage in this activity "day and night." Neither time nor the soul is split in the life of the righteous. What is revealed by the light of day is practiced in the darkness of night, the private and the public are one, something usually not true of those who are engaged in nefarious activities, especially those people, public officials, respected burghers, who try to hide their corruption. This unity is further stressed by the ambiguous pronoun in the second part of the verse—*his* teaching. To be sure, the referent is most likely God, but only a moment before, the same pronoun, *his*, referred to the devotee—"his desire." Implied is a unity of the activity of the righteous person and God's own intent. The words that the righteous utter, his teaching, is one with God's.

The first two verses of the psalm have presented us with a description of the contrasting lives of the righteous and the evildoers. It has opened up worlds through a poetic concreteness yet with conciseness of language. The next two sentences offer contrasting images for the consequences of these paths, and the poet advances the contrast of good and evil through the telling use of two powerful agricultural metaphors.

> For he will be as a tree planted astride streams
> bearing fruit in season,
> its leaves never shriveling—
> everything thriving.

First, there is a four-part development of the metaphor describing the fate of the righteous as a fertile, long-lived tree: firmly planted, bearing fruit in season, not desiccated, a truly successful growth. In the description of the tree that never hibernates but is always lush, we are presented with the most elaborate metaphor within the psalm. We have gone from a three-line description of the ways of the wicked to a tightly packed two-line description of the inner life of the righteous to an outward explosion of the rich life of that righteous person. Most biblical poetic sentences contain just two clauses—the simplest form of parallelism; somewhat less frequently, a sentence will contain three clauses; four is the rarest form. Thus, the verse displays an exuberant description of permanence and fecundity, emphasizing the fullness of blessing reserved for the righteous which is the theme struck by the very first word of the psalm, "*Ashrei*/Blessed . . ." The constancy of blessing is consequent on the constancy of devotion. The never dying, ever fruitful tree, always flourishing for it lives by the side of flowing water, depicts the fullness of God's blessing, a life always assured of divine nourishment.

In Hebrew, subjects are often dropped from clauses, and that is the case here in the fourth and last phrase "everything thriving." The thriving could refer to *he,* the righteous, or *it,* the tree; that is, the phrase could just as well be translated "And all that *it* does thrives," referring back to the tree, or "And all that *he* does thrives," referring to the righteous. The ambiguity of the referent ensures that readers understand both the image and its referent are one and the same. Metaphor and reality meld so that one does not know which is which. The righteous have become like the most flourishing of trees: permanent, solid, sustained through all seasons, prolific. Equally, the appeal to an image in nature communicates to us the feeling that the fate of the righteous is as inherent in the world as the laws of vegetation. Just as God, the creator, assures blessing in nature, and outcomes are predictable (trees receiving abundant water will flourish), so too human society will reflect God's order: the righteous shall flourish. A law of life is at work that is as true of human fate as of the natural world.

The verbal profuseness describing the fecundity of the righteous is now set off by the startling phrase that introduces the next parallel sentence:

> Not so the wicked.

Here we have no verb or object, just the negation of the subject. The flourishing of the righteous elaborated with rhetorical rococo is now contrasted with the absolute rejection of the wicked signaled by the simple and bare phrasing of this line. Having no verb, evil is banished into nonexistence.

In the second clause of the sentence, this negation is given metaphoric content: they "are only like chaff, tossed by the wind." The wicked have no weight, they are blown away by the wind. They are so light, so ephemeral, so easily manipulated by the winds of time, that they hardly have existence. As opposed to the righteous who will be firmly rooted, the wicked will be seen to lack any substance. The image of the chaff blown away by the wind is borrowed from everyday life in a society that is primarily agricultural, quickly conveying the idea of waste product—every farmer has to be rid of the chaff in order to have something useful from the harvest: the wheat kernel. Equally, the chaff is an outer shell that the passerby sees all through the summer as the planted crop grows, but at harvest time it is not the outer shell but the kernel, hidden through the growing season, that then produces the flour that sustains human life. It is the hidden kernel that is valuable, cherished; the shell, the element that until now has displayed itself, is, in the end just tossed aside. Though the wicked have seemingly ruled the day, at the time of reckoning, at the harvest, it is they who will pass into utter insignificance.

The temporal considerations we have just remarked on are not incidental. Currently, it may look as though the righteous do not have the upper hand in society. But know: as the stalk of wheat rises, a passerby does not see the kernel, but surely that is the object of the plant's growth. Those in power may have their day in the sun, but soon they will be cut off and thrown away. The concreteness of the image makes us assent to its truth, and makes us feel that the ideal reality being described is more real than the present concrete reality.

Psalms are fluid in their use of tenses and here the change of tenses from the past tense of the first verse of the psalm to the future articulated in these verses deliberately conveys temporal ambiguity. The future tense in biblical Hebrew is also used to describe a continuous present activity, and in these verses it is hard to tell whether the agricultural metaphors describe an ongoing present activity or a future imagined as becoming present. The change of tenses though allows for an easy transition to the ending, which is surely an imagined future. But the fluidity of tenses allows us to understand that this future is as sure as any past action.

> So, the wicked will not stand up in court
> nor sinners in the assembly of the righteous

In the first part of the psalm we have been conscious of the variety of groups of sinners, contrasted with the singleness of the person of faith: "Blessed is the one who . . ."—it is the lonely individual who is described, and that isolated feeling is reinforced in the image of the one seeking to do right sitting at home at night studying, alone with his book, reading by candlelight. But now, in the time of judgment, the righteous have discovered each other: it is they who are an assembly; the endtime not only finds the wicked guilty but creates the condition for the "assembly of the righteous." The corrupt had occupied the public places, they had "standing," while the righteous had to preserve their faith in the privacy of their hearts. Finally, the righteous are a public, able to stand together; it is the sinner who will now have no company:

> nor sinners in the assembly of the righteous.

The image of negation begun with the metaphor of the harvest is now given finality. The righteous will now find each other and form a congregation, and the cabal of those who oppose righteousness, who once thought of themselves as having true community, will now find themselves as chaff, separated out. Even more, God, who until this time has only been alluded to and had only been hinted at as the mysterious hand behind nature, will now appear in the midst of the righteous.

> for Adonai knows the way of the just
> but the way of the wicked will be lost.

The use of the word "know" in the first half of this sentence calls out for some explanation. Isn't the point that God also knows of the path of the wicked, and therefore will surely punish the sinner? Is it not the case that God knows all? Here though, "knowing" is used in the sense of having a relationship, of being intimate with. It is not a superficial acknowledgment of recognition, the way we might be asked if we have ever met so-and-so and we respond, "I know him," but rather this is a constant presence that is the mark of true friendship—an intimate and deep involvement. Interestingly, the New Jewish Publication Society version here translates the Hebrew word *know* as "cherish." To cherish and to know are states of mind and heart. The righteous person was distinguished by purity of heart, and it is through the intimacy of relatedness, the understandings of the heart, that God will reward the good. The righteous have been distinguished through the lonely faithfulness of their soul, through their meditative study, and they will be rewarded by God's "knowing" them, by a meeting of the human's inner life and the inner life of God.

But something else has happened here as well. This last sentence contains a twofold mention of the "way," and the two clauses delineate their opposing fates. God's knowing the way of the righteous is certainly an assurance of its permanence, even of its eternality, while the way of the wicked will prove to be no way at all. The first sentence of the psalm introduced us to the way of the wicked, and we saw the contrast between the way of the wicked and the inner life of the righteous. Now we learn that the way of the wicked is no way, that it has no lasting value, and that it is like a track in the sand wiped away by the wind. In contradistinction to the way of the wicked, the faithfulness of the righteous constitutes the only path that has permanence and lasting worth. In the end, the way of the heart will win out. If one were to give a title to this poem it might be "Which way?" And the last sentence constitutes the final and absolute response to this question. Faithfulness is permanent. Corrupt power, the forces which are seemingly dominant, are illusory and passing.

This last thought is emphasized through the choice of verbs in the two final clauses:

> For Adonai knows the way of the just,
> but the way of the wicked will be lost.

Although this last Hebrew word of the psalm is literally translated as *to be lost*, its more emphatic meaning is *destroyed*, for to be lost is to no longer be found, and therefore no longer to have existence. God's knowing the righteous is exactly the opposite of this nonexistence: God's entering into a relationship with them gives life and permanent vitality to those who are in the relationship. There is in fact only one way that has permanence.

It is frequently the case that the wonder of psalmic rhetoric is its ability to make the leap between the harsh reality we encounter and the imagined world of divine presence. Poetic art can paint a picture foreclosed to rational analysis. After all, religious themes often exist in an in-between world—religious belief asserts a vision of "truth" that reaches beyond encountered reality. The grace of the psalmic art is that it can help make the world of the imagination, of belief, real—it can make present a wished-for future. Poetry can paint this imagined reality better than prose. It is poetic art that fleshes out the central ideas of this psalm and makes them believable.

By the end of this first psalm the author has taken us through quite a journey. The surety of God's ultimate presence and justice has offered consolation for whatever tribulations the good person may currently suffer as wrongdoers strut about exercising power in society. The poet's pen paints a different picture than contemporary experience, and art has overcome reality: belief has triumphed through the painting of a word picture.

That takes us back to the very first words of the psalm which spoke of blessing.

> Blessed is the person . . .

It is the one phrase that does not follow the parallel structure. It is the opening phrase of the psalm and hangs in the air hovering over each subsequent thought. In reality, it is the phrase necessary to complete the thought of each of the clauses composing the first sentence, which ought to read:

> Blessed is the person who has not pursued the counsel of the wicked
> and blessed is the person who has not stood with sinners on their way
> and blessed is the person who has not sat with the indolent.

Sometimes, the psalmic poet will rejoice in such repetitions and the same word or phrase will appear in clause after clause; so emphasized, the idea is driven home.[3] A certain musical rhythm is set in motion by such repetitions and though it might make for boring prose, it can provide the necessary repetitive beat punctuating the music of a poem or song. Here though, the nonrepetition of the opening word hands its care over to us, puts us in charge of keeping it in mind precisely because it is not spoken again. We are responsible for remembering the phrase, and the strong parallel structure of the clauses makes it inevitable that we continue to hear the blessing promised to the righteous even as it is unspoken. As we read the second and third clauses we understand that we are being instructed how to behave, and that the blessing of the opening phrase is meant to contrast with all the varieties of wickedness. This structure having forced us to remain aware of the blessing of the righteous throughout the first sentence, makes us mindful of it throughout the poem. Indeed, this unrepeated word is held in our thoughts till we reach the very end of the poem when we read the last word: "lost." On the one hand, there is the promise of blessing, implying ongoing life, permanence, fruitfulness; and on the other hand, loss, destruction, disappearance. The poetic structure makes us hear the first word

---

3. Psalm 32, for instance, uses this repetition of *ashrei* ("blessed"). There the dual repetition emphasizes the fact that the poet feels the lack of blessing.

even as we read the last. We may come to feel that blessing is the treasure of God, withheld till the time appropriate for the reward. The blessing, which is so assuredly stated as the opening word of the poem, is held in abeyance till the end of the psalm but is most assuredly there, always. It is there in the whisper of the mind. The blessing is a promise not yet achieved.

Through the use of rhetorical arts, the hidden God has been made manifest to the faithful. Trust that God's hand, unseen now, will be made visible—it is always at work. Trust in God who is the hidden kernel of life. *Blessing*—the Hebrew word conveys contentment, spiritual richness, inner happiness and outer fruitfulness—which is now perhaps hidden, will ultimately be manifest; this is God's promise. It is not surprising that, recited throughout the generations, these words have served to comfort devotees, for by reciting these words an alternate vision of reality than we may have experienced is convincingly enunciated and affirmed.

But for us moderns—and perhaps for many previous generations—the view of the psalmist, the sharp contrast of good and evil, may be problematic. Is the world really bifurcated between those who are righteous and those who align with sin? Aren't our motives frequently ambiguous? Who has not sinned? Who has not been tossed and turned by a variety of inclinations? Are we to be counted among the righteous though we hear the ambivalence of own inner voices, and recognize the imperfections of our own behavior? Or am I to suffer the fate of the wicked, for I know that I am no saint! Where is my place in this worldview?

It is true that at some historical moments the contrasting opposition between good and evil is obvious. If you were a Jew on the run in Nazi Poland, who was good and who was evil was clear. The peasant you met either turned you in, slammed the door in your face, or saved you. Perhaps the psalm speaks to such moments of clarity.

But most of life is not lived with those absolute choices. Most of us live in a muddled world in which we would like to see ourselves as doing good but end up being caught in the vortex of personal desire and satisfaction. Motive turns out to be complex: ambition, authority, power when intended for good purpose, are easily consumed by selfish ends. Even those whom we may consider evil do good: what are we to make of robber barons who become great philanthropists? How are we to account for public officials, even presidents, who may accomplish much public good but whose private lives are despicable? The images of Psalm 1 do not admit of moral ambiguity or of the finitude of all human behavior. Who can stand up to a strict final accounting?

Perhaps, in some measure, that is the revelatory power of psalms like this one: they call us to a sense of the absolute usually missing in our lives, they awaken us to an alternative perspective where what is demanded of us is that we not excuse ourselves but see our lives as having the possibility of clarity and unity. Psalm 1 is a poem that insists that there are obvious standards of judgment.

This psalm, then, stands outside us and calls to us—awakes us to self-reflection. The poem exhorts us to hear the call contained in biblical teaching, the word that calls to us from beyond ourselves, but which equally arises in our heart of hearts. It is because the poet seeks to call us to that which is hidden, to make explicit and obvious that which for many of us is a struggle, that may give this elegant psalm some of its power. It is this call which turns the psalm into a kind of revelation—a word coming from outside that gives voice to our innermost conscience. The psalm asks us to look at the good and evil battling within us, to see the inclination to domination and spoilation as well as the wish to do good as a part of each of us and beckons us to choose.[4]

Other psalms give voice to inner doubts and ambivalence. As I have said, especially in this post-Freudian age, we experience ourselves as conflicted human beings. Few of us think of our lives as being pure. For me, it is in fact those psalms that acknowledge our inadequacy and yet nevertheless seek to face God that provide the most touching prayer-filled moments; but this psalm, in its singlemindedness, has a simplicity about it that exerts its own pull. One can admire the clear message expressed in Psalm 1, especially because it is so artfully presented, while yet reaching for expressions that would more closely match our inner ambivalence.

4. Saadiah Gaon, the first great Jewish commentator on psalms, saw the book of Psalms as a second revelation of the Torah. (The fact that Psalms is divided into five books probably spurred the metaphor.) See Simon, *Four Approachces to the Book of Psalms*, 1–57.

2

Psalm 19

Prayer

EVERY GREAT POEM IS a journey. We are different at the end than we were at the beginning—there are new realizations, new ways of understanding our lives, new perspectives with which to view the world. The poem has given us a different consciousness, and we can be so full of new thoughts that we may not realize how the poet has manipulated this magic carpet. Psalm 1 moves from present to future and sees the life of the righteous fulfilled in an end-time whose imagining is made fully present through poetic art. In contrast, Psalm 19 remarks on creation and is filled with rhetorical devices that communicate the experience of God's continuous presence. But though in Psalm 1 the devotee finally finds his justification, as we reach the end of Psalm 19 the poet will express feelings of disquiet, of being out of place, of being found wanting. Indeed, the psalm will begin to explicitly raise the very issue we found problematic in Psalm 1: the ambivalence that lies in the heart of the devotee. The note of disquiet with which Psalm 19 ends begins to undo the singlemindedness asserted in the first psalm.

But first a literary note that will help us as we turn to Psalm 19. When I am puzzled by a psalm, when I can't quite figure out what the psalm is saying, what territory it has traversed, I try to analyze the divisions of the poem—what are the stanzas in this psalm. If I can determine that, then I can see in what direction the poem is developing, I can understand its argument, its movement. Stanzas are the stages in the journey—the way a poet moves us along to a new vision, a transformed understanding, or a different set of emotions than those with which we began. It is the placement of stanza upon stanza that moves us to a new viewpoint. With each stanza we enter the world of new metaphor, different time, or other emotion. We just saw, for instance, that Psalm 1 had three distinct parts, each offering a contrast between the righteous and the sinner. The argument of the poem—current observations and realities contrasted with future transformation—is displayed as a movement from one stanza to the next.

The stanzas in Psalm 19 are so distinct from each other that we will have no difficulty in identifying the stages, though many will experience an initial difficulty in seeing the connection between the parts. A close reading, though, will show how attention to the poem's internal divisions unlocks meaning—how building upon stages of development, a psalm can gain power.

PSALM 19

1   From the conductor,
A Davidic Song,

2   The heavens recount God's glory;
the sky proclaims, "The work of His hands."

3   One day pours out speech to another,
night informs a next night—

4   There is no speech,
and there is no expression
whose sounds go unheard.

5   Their waves travel throughout the world,
their message to the ends of the earth.

6   In their midst, He placed a tent for the sun,
who is like a groom coming forth from the chamber,
like an athlete, joyously running his course.

7   At one end of heaven it rises,
its circuit reaches the other end;
and nothing escapes its heat.

8   The teaching of Adonai is perfect,
renewing life.

The decrees of Adonai are enduring,
making wise the simple.

9 The precepts of Adonai are just,
   gladdening the heart.

   The instruction of Adonai is lucid,
   lighting up the eyes.

10 The fear of Adonai is pure,
   abiding forever.

   The judgments of Adonai are true,
   righteous altogether—

11 more desirable than gold,
   more than shiny metal;
   sweeter than honey,
   than the drippings of the comb.

12 And Your servant is illumined by them;
   obeying them is of great consequence.

13 Who can be aware of errors?
   Cleanse me of hidden ones,

14 separate Your servant from sinners,

   let me remain innocent,
   that I be cleansed of grave offense.

15 Be pleased with the words of my mouth,
   and the intonations of my heart, expressed to You
   Adonai, my rock and my redeemer.

In this psalm, we move from nature, to God, to the human. The first verses offer a graceful description of the natural world focusing on the heavens, including an extended metaphor centering on the sun. The second stanza, verses 8 to 11, is a paean to God's teaching; it is an ecstatic elegy to Torah, each line competing with the next for superlatives. The last section is the personal reflection of the psalmist, beginning with a brooding meditation and ending in prayer.

The problem of this psalm is not to understand where the stanza divisions occur, though there might be some minor difference of opinion on whether the second stanza break occurs after verse 11 or after verse 12, but rather how the sections connect to form one poem—how this poem constitutes a single journey. On first reading, the parts may seem disparate, disconnected.

The connecting link is speech, and critically the poem revolves around the different kinds of speech each section defines. The opening first three verses of the poem are filled with metaphors of speech and sound: heavens recount, sky proclaims, days communicate, night informs, and all this is heard. It is as if the music of the spheres were a concert we could attend. Nature is not silent, but full of reverberations—if we but listen. There is a surprising conceit as not only space (the heavenly spheres) voice praise of God, but time itself tells a story: one day converses with another. Speech is everywhere, though we humans may not hear it; the chorus is a tribute to God, the author of creation. It was God's speech that created the world, and in turn the universe is filled with sound. Yet who listens to this performance? Other heavenly bodies? God?

The question is not an extraneous one but is central to the summary sentence of the section, the fourth verse:

> There is no speech,
> and there is no expression
> whose sounds go unheard.

Here we are presented with a deliberately unstated subject: who is it, then, doing the listening? It is, after all, the psalmist who is admiring the heavens. It is the poet who looks to the heavens and, seeing the patterns of nature, recognizes the God beyond. It is as if the author is saying: all you have to do is look, and you will hear the voice of nature crying out with its design. Each of us has had the experience of being struck by nature: a moment in which we admire its harmony, when walking by the sea or stopping in a forest we may listen for the beat of pulsating life—the beating of the waves, the squawking of birds, the rustling of wind and leaves. The psalm recalls for us those moments, beckoning us to hear that music once again—to hear the interstices of nature whispering its song.

Nature's speech is, of course, different from human speech: it is there for the listening, though it never speaks in articulated language, its message transcending human language. As Martin Buber, the twentieth-century Jewish philosopher, so aptly put it in a different context, the speech of nature "is below the lintel" of human accessibility—we can sense it is there, but in a way quite different than articulated words. The poet invites us to overhear what can be listened to and so allows us to see the vastness, the grandeur, the beauty of nature, which we might have forgotten even as we understand that we can never hear it in its fullness. "There is nothing which goes unheard": even the silent speaking of nature hidden from the human is attended to by an anonymous listener who guarantees that all will be noticed. We listen in on some of the sounds around us, we peer heaven-ward, but there is a vast beyond that only the ear of God can hear.[1]

Our capacity to discover a song in nature points to a beyond which is not visibly present, and it can make us aware of the unseen God who creates, the hidden God who listens. Modern physics knows that deep inside the most petrified wood tiny parts of atoms move, and the seeming stillness is only possible because of this movement; similarly, the ancients' view was that the skies might be still, but they were never silent. There is something that stirs in the so-called silence of the universe, and that stirring points to God. Just as what is seemingly silent in nature is filled with sound, so too the seemingly empty universe is filled with God's hovering presence. That presence is felt precisely by not being mentioned directly in these verses. In this part of the poem only the generic word for God, *El*, is used—not the personal, relational four letter name of Adonai. In this part of the poem God hovers in the background: the psalmist alludes to God as an anonymous third person, maintaining God's mystery, even as God's handiwork, and therefore God's reassuring presence, is acknowledged.

In the end, it is that listening quality of the Divine which will offer comfort to the psalmist, for God listens to all things, even the hardly expressed yearnings of our hearts. But then there is an underside to that constant presence which can be unsettling, though the poet, at the beginning, makes no allusion to it: if everything can be heard, if everything has consequences, then what of our own stray thoughts—or more precisely, our own inner conflicted beings? What of the thoughts and desires that hover around the forbidden? After all, we are the children of Adam and Eve, who were expelled from the Garden because of overweening desire. This issue of human fallibility will emerge as a problem later in the poem, but for the moment the poet holds it in abeyance. The image of God in this first stanza is beneficent, if only by proxy—seen through creation, God's handiwork, which we daily apprehend.

Surprisingly, the psalmist jumps immediately from the image of voice and speech whose sound is heard by God to the figure of the sun moving through its course in the heavens. The psalmist does not want to linger with the implications of hiddenness but rather indicates an obvious presence. The sun nourishes us and the rest of the earth, day in and day out, endlessly.

---

1. Interestingly, scientists recently hypothesized that the sun emits sounds but they are caught in the sun's energy field and cannot escape its gravitational field. Now, scientists have developed instruments to listen in to this internal speech of the sun.

We live from its rays that reach everywhere. There is no place on land or sea that conceals itself from the sun (just as the song of the spheres could not be hidden). So the opening stanza concerning nature concludes the sun metaphor with the line

> and nothing escapes its heat.

This ending to verse 7 parallels the ending to verse 4 which contended that no speech goes unheard. The music of the spheres is imagined, but the heat of the sun is felt. What was said of invisible speech is validated by sight. The wonderful circuit of the sun, which illuminates what would otherwise be dark, which dispels shadows, provides the heat that is the energy for all of life—a stand-in for the constant care of the Creator. In this first stanza, while God remains in the background, all of nature issues in a speaking that points to God's presence, God's care; God's presence is felt through the agency of the sun with its life-giving power. When we experience the heat of the sun that nourishes us and is the blessing creation offers each day, we are really experiencing God's gift.

The next verses begin the second stanza which constitutes a distinct break in imagery and rhetoric from the first. The subject matter totally changes: from the wonder of creation the poet now moves to a description of the preciousness of God's revelation, not nature's speech but God's own speech, not the word of God hidden within creation but the words that God spoke directly.

And instead of being a presence hovering in the background, God is now mentioned in each verse and the name of God that is used is the personal one, the four-letter name that God revealed to Moses repeated here in each line.

Also, this second section incorporates a distinct stylistic shift. We are treated to a series of six definitions and descriptions of God's word: "The law of God is . . ." "The testimonies of God are . . ." In the Hebrew, there is a staccato pattern in each of these phrases: three words, followed by two words, forming a litany, in which the individual elements matter less than the rhythmic piling up of metaphors expressing the power of God's word to give strength to the human. Though less pronounced, this pattern is easily experienced by the English reader, as well.

It is interesting to think of this second stanza not simply as consti-tuting an abrupt shift but as somehow spurred by an intimate metaphoric connection to what has come before. God's words are like the sun, which every day, illuminates the earth, refreshing it, rising anew, till the end of time; Torah offers us clarity as we walk through life.

Yet the contrast with the previous image is surely there: God's speech is explicit, the God behind nature must be surmised. Revelation provides us with so much more than nature's glories—explicit direction for our lives and the means for a direct relation with God.

Verse 11, the seventh declaration of this stanza, breaks the pattern established in the previous six, much as the description of the seventh day in the creation story strays from the linguistic pattern describing the first six days in the first chapter of Genesis:

> more desirable than gold,
> more than shiny metal;
> sweeter than honey,
> than the drippings of the comb.

There is no subject stated in these sentences and we presume that they apply to the totality of what has come before, the previous six enumerations. Just as the seventh day may be seen not as a new day of creation but as a consummation of the work of six days, an expression of fullness, so this last declaration looks back on all that has been enunciated and finds it superlative. What we have in this last utterance is a burst of praise, clauses expressing the overwhelming joy in God's word, God's revelation as the ultimate good. Six days are devoted to creation, but the seventh has a special connection to God: it contains holiness and blessing, for it is the sum of all that has gone before. This seventh metaphor for God's revelation describes an ultimate worth, the sweetest nourishment.

Unlike the second stanza, which breaks abruptly with the first stanza both in form and content, the transition to the third stanza occurs without a sense of interruption: "Your servant is illumined by them." The referent of 'them' is clearly Torah, God's teaching, which has been the subject of the second stanza; Torah is alluded to by a pronoun rather than named, thus forcing us to refer back to what was just enunciated. This new stanza enters by compelling us to link up to what has gone before. (Linguistically, too, there is a word repetition: *rav*—"much"—found in verse 11 is also found in verse 12 forming yet another link between the two sections.) The link attempts to establish a progression in which the human can be placed: nature sounds its song, God utters the words of Torah and human beings speak—nature's song contains a hint of God's word inhering in it, the word which created it; Torah is distinctly God's speech; and the human is created in the image of God—the manifestation of the divine image is speech, consciousness. But if nature's speech is hidden, and God's word is manifest, the human is made up of a curious combination of the two—we human beings can speak in a more articulate way than nature can, but the promptings of our hearts, which are the sources of our speech, are hidden even from us. Consciousness is explicit, the unconscious is hidden. The human is a mixture of hiddenness and revelation.

The first word of this last stanza is a connective, the Hebrew *gam*, meaning "also," and here simply translated as "and." It is an "and" which both connects and separates. Like nature and like God, the human can utter sounds. It is, in fact, human speech that makes us God-like. But the human word, unlike either nature's song or God's speech, introduces the possibility of sin. The circuit of the sun may be flawless, and the sun may be described as a perfect athlete, an absolute hero; Torah is certainly perfect speech, but the human is always caught in an inner war—conflicting internal voices battle for the heart of each person.

So the entrance of human speech, for all it attempts to connect with what has gone before, brings us to a radical break in creation. Our speech may not lead to wholeness and blessing, but rather make us conscious of our individual needs, it can be expressive of our envy and jealousy, our hurt, our desire, our felt lack and what we say may not even express the truth but intentionally falsify. Human speech contains neither the naive purity of nature nor the completed self-consciousness of God. It is a mixture of the two—it can be a divine instrument or it can introduce the conversations of Babel, the revolt against the received order of creation. As another psalmist will say using a different image, we are but little lower than angels, but we are also no different than animals. It is the fact of admixture that makes us so complex, so interesting, so dangerous, even to ourselves, for we hardly know what we think, what darkness we contain, and yet we can speak, like the divine.

And so with the introduction of the human, we are greeted with the introduction of the personal *I* and enter into the first troubled moment in the psalm. Verse 13 reads:

> And Your servant is illumined by them;
> Obeying them is of great consequence.
>
> Who can be aware of errors?
> Cleanse me of hidden ones,

On the one hand, we can be "illumined." God's light hinted at in the metaphor of the sun and described as the fullness of the teaching in the second stanza can permeate our inner life. But we know all too well that we are not like God—the light of our self-reflection does not reach everywhere, there is much about ourselves that we do not understand. Notoriously, there are parts of our inner life that remain hidden even from ourselves. It is in fact our lack of omniscience, our inability to be God-like, that creates our humanity and our terrible sense of separation from God. Our mental life is a constant argument with ourselves, and our dream world teaches us that there is so much in our heart for which we cannot account. If God truly sees and hears all, then surely God has penetrated the heart of the human, knows our inner contradictions, our inner debates, our dreams and nightmares, the terrors of our soul that we are too afraid to articulate even to ourselves. Most times, we can hardly discern our own motives: Are we helpful to someone because we care? Because we need them? Because we want to be thought well of? Much of our waking life is spent questioning ourselves, controlling our jealousies, reigning in our competitiveness. God knows all our self-doubts, the constant inner war for our soul, and so would never find us innocent. Even the best of us cannot control the unpredictable promptings of the heart. We can never think of ourselves as pure and righteous. God's ear listens in to this division in our heart; haven't we agreed that nothing escapes God's vision? And what does God make of us?

While the first part of the psalm is permeated by the consciousness of the word of God embedded in nature, and enunciated through the daily wonders of the world, and the second part is a paean to God's own speaking, God's revealed word, the psalmist has now turned to a third kind of speech, the utterances of the heart.[2] Knowing how subject we are to inner forces of which we are hardly aware, we need to take care of how we live.

> separate your servant from sinners,
> let me remain innocent,
> that I be cleansed of grave offense.

Let me not be put into situations where I be tempted to do something wrong. Out of anger, attacked by enemies, I may act in a way that violates God's law. Even though a response may be justified, nevertheless, I may

---

2. It was Michael Fishbane who first showed me the way this psalm is made up of three different kinds of speech. I appreciate his critical insight so important to understanding this psalm.

act disproportionately. Or perhaps the poet is arguing that even the proportional response, though justified, is always destructive and therefore a blight on God's creation. Keep me away from every temptation to act in a way not reflective of the divine creative power.

And so the last line of the psalm is a prayer:

> Be pleased with the words of my mouth,
> and the intonations of my heart, expressed to You
> Adonai, my rock and my redeemer.

We humans are able to sing many songs, say many things. One of the kinds of speech of which we are capable is prayer, and that prayer can include a plea for forgiveness. What we are left with at the end of this poem is supplication. Human speech can turn into a facing toward God, and that is the special religious gift of humanity's speaking. We may be bifurcated, but out of our inner conflicts can be fashioned something that neither earlier forms of speech are capable of—the introspective moment of regret which is the approach to God. While the first stanza can refer to God in a generic sense and allude to God in third person, and the second can use the familiar name of God, this third stanza introduces an *I* who speaks to a *You*. It is Your servant who asks to cleanse me. Prayer is the moment when speech becomes a conversation with God. And it is this speech that is redemptive—it can establish a deeper relationship than any of the kinds of speech alluded to earlier. The human introduces speech as conversation, marked here by the acknowledgment of difference and the expression of regret.

And conversation with God is prayer. Thus the poet says: may my speech be worthy speech, may it, too, reflect the Creator. Not incidentally, the word "cleanse" is repeated twice in this moment of prayer. Though my words are broken, may God receive them as whole. The other side of God's seeing into my heart is that God knows how much I intend to do good, though in my imperfection, actions and words may emerge that are flawed. May my voice sound to You as perfect as the other sounds enunciated in the world. May the words of prayer, of hope and wish, be as acceptable to You as the seamless praise which nature offers. May you consider me as pure as all your other creations. Thus, human speech turns toward God and asks for a response, that its speech be received, that it be interpreted by the listener, that it be understood—just as everything in nature is heard.

The very last word of the psalm, "my redeemer" (the Hebrew is one word) is not simply an incidental appellation for God, for it is God as redeemer who forgives, who cares, who loves, who raises us up. Redemption is the ongoing goal of God's creation and revelation; redemption is the final end of creation, the completion of creation. God can transform our incomplete gift, our attempt to approach the holy, into a moment of fullness. God can find acceptable all that we do imperfectly. God can lift up the offering of our hearts.

The God who creates nature, the God who instructs us, is the same God who is capable of understanding the sincere, though sometimes misstated, plaint of the heart. Creation, now incomplete because of the rent in the human soul, can be made whole again, can be completed, as God faces the human, hears our speech, and forgives us. Prayer, the articulation of the human heart, has the power to effect this turning, it can initiate the reconciliation of God and creation—then I, in all my so very human self-contradiction, may be affirmed. God, who knows all and sees all, can understand my intent and find me, like the rest of creation, good.

It is precisely because the devotee links his or her voice with that of nature and that of God's own speech that the plea for the hearing of the human voice derives its special poignancy. The contradiction inherent in the human condition is understood as a religious problem needing resolution because the psalmist has so carefully delineated the nature of speech in the first two stages of the poem. Were we to have only the last stanza, the prayer of the devoted poet, we would be left with an ordinary moment, a simple prayer of forgiveness. The presence of the other stanzas of the poem enlarges the author's prayer. The fissure within the devotee is contrasted with the perfection of nature and of God's speech. It is that contrast which creates the poignancy embedded in the prayer. Yet, it is the assurances conveyed in the earlier part of the poem that equally communicate the possibility of the devotee being received in wholeness by God. The first two stanzas have celebrated God's continuous caring involvement, God's ongoing presence in the world, and that belief creates the ground for hoping for the redemptive moment, for insisting that the prayer of the heart will be heard and be received. The God of creation, the God of revelation, must also be the God of redemption, and redemption is here seen as God affirming the human in all of his or her self-contradiction. The variety of speech has progressed through the psalm until, finally, even the imperfect human word can be included with the speaking of nature and of God.

The author of Psalm 1 may have depicted the righteous as single minded; the poet writing Psalm 19 recognizes the ambivalence characteristic of human beings. Human self-consciousness is ever aware of the disruption the human causes in creation. The psalmist portrays human ambivalence as the very source of prayer and artfully asserts that, for good and for ill, God hears all.

3

Psalm 8

Between Heaven and Earth

WHAT DOES IT MEAN to be human? Where do we fit in the scheme of creation? Psalm 19 began to explore human difference, our separation from the rest of creation. Once we notice the difference between us and the rest of nature, we begin to ask larger questions, set in motion, if you will, with our fall from Eden: Are we spiritual beings, or are we more analogous to animals? Are we really only paltry, weak, vulnerable beings subject to death, quickly passing from the scene, created from the dust of the earth and returning to it? What is the nature of our power? These are the questions that concern the psalmist in Psalm 8.

PSALM 8

1   From the conductor: on the gittith.[1] A Davidic Psalm.

2   Adonai—our master—
How grand is Your name throughout the earth,
You, whose splendor is displayed on the heavens:

3   From the mouth of infants and sucklings
You have founded strength against Your besiegers
quieting enemy and avenger.

4   When I behold Your heavens, the work of Your fingers,
the moon and stars that You set in place,

---

1. The meaning of this term has been lost.

5   what are human beings that You have been mindful of them,[2]
the descendants of Adam that You have taken note of them?

6   For You have made them little less than divine
and adorned them with honor and glory;

7   You have anointed them rulers over Your handiwork,
laying it all at their feet:

8   Sheep and oxen, all of them,
along with the animals on the range,

9   the birds of the heavens, the fish of the sea,
whatever travels the paths of the seas.

10   Adonai—our master—
How grand is Your name throughout the earth!

Psalms are poems, not works of philosophy. They don't convey their meaning by announcing a linear argument. They convey their message through their evocative power. So before dealing with the questions that are the subject of this biblical poem, a word about the particular poetics of this psalm.

A psalmist usually provides us with considerable hints of how we might view the poem as we step back and look over the whole. For instance, one of the important devices the psalmist employs to make us see the journey is the use of a frame—scholars sometimes call this device an *inclusio*—an opening line and closing line, which play off each other. The clearest example of such a frame is the exact repetition of the same line at the opening and closing. It is a technique that especially compels us to look at the road we have traveled and forces us, as a final act of reading, to put the poem together again as one piece. The beginning and the end echo each other in such a clear way that we are compelled to try to see both the opening and exit of the tunnel in one glance. But we are different at the end than at the beginning for having traveled the space between the two.

Psalm 8 uses the device of an exact repetition of its first and last line and it is interesting to note how different the line feels at these two moments: "Adonai—our master—How grand is Your name throughout the earth!" Clearly the poet intended us to see the intervening lines as a demonstration of the initial proposition that is "proven" by the end and

2. I have changed the Hebrew from the singular to the plural in order to avoid having to offer a gender specific translation. In Genesis 1, Adam is clearly both male and female. Similarly Genesis 5:2 says "God created them, male and female, blessed them and called them "Adam" on the day that God created them.

therefore has the right of reassertion. But what we ought to see is that by the time we get to the end of the poem, we realize that the opening phrase is deeper, subtler, more powerful than we could have possibly comprehended in the beginning, and that therefore our experience of the first and last lines is in fact different. It is the experience of that difference that is the message of the poem; it is the explication of that difference that marks the journey of meaning on which the poem takes us.

> Adonai—our master—
> How grand is Your name throughout the earth,
> You, whose splendor is displayed on the heavens:

This opening verse of the psalm, so seemingly simple and straightforward, hints at several problematic elements of biblical theology. Naming is peculiarly associated with that aspect of the human that is imitative of God. In all of nature it is only humanity that operates with consciousness, that is, with the ability to name. Naming is the initial human act in the Garden of Eden: Adam names all the animals that pass before him. The acknowledgment of God's name on earth, the acknowledgment of God as creator, is the singular gift the human can return to God. When the human names God on earth, brings God within earthly discourse, celebrates God through speech, he or she truly ushers in the kingdom of God. This naming is not only a matter of speaking the word—the name of God—but of celebrating God with one's whole being, through all of one's acts: the establishment of an ideal, making of earth a heavenly kingdom. Whenever the Bible speaks of God's name as spreading over the earth, the metaphor describes this mirroring of heaven and earth, the establishment of God's kingdom here on earth, which the Bible frequently identifies with the rule of justice and goodness. When humanity sounds the name of God in full-throated chorus, Eden is reentered, for the ideal world is reestablished.

But God's name will be one with life on earth only in a culminating moment, an endtime. The world we are presented with in daily existence is not like this—it is no kingdom of heaven. The reality we meet does not present us with a triumphant God but rather with forces of good and evil at war with each other: justice does not predominate but has to be fought for; goodness is not rewarded and often leads to suffering; life is not only a gift and a blessing but is often filled with the tragic. Heaven and earth are experienced as separate realms.

So the opening lines of the poem assert an understanding contradicted by our own immediate human experience of reality. Our sense of the world is not of God's name being ubiquitously present. The opening line following the poem's frame becomes an ironic statement of the problem of the poem. God's splendor is written in the heavens. One has only to look up and see how glorious the universe is, how vast, how subtle, how ordered. God rules the heavens—would that were equally true on earth! The earth ought to be a mirror of the heavens; it ought to reflect God's reign. But life on earth is unjust, sometimes painful, often full of conflict and even violence. The notable discordancy between the ideal picture of heaven and the reality of existence is the tension that disturbs all religious life. God then is visible in the heavens, but on earth . . . ?

In the next lines we hear about these antagonistic forces—"besiegers," "enemies," "avengers." These are forces that oppose God's rule, those who believe in other gods, those now in power who are corrupt, those who are unjust. The good is not triumphant but under siege; justice is undermined by its enemies; battles have to be fought to defend the faithful.

> From the mouth of infants and sucklings
> You have founded strength against Your besiegers
> quieting enemy and avenger.

The initial contradiction now gains in intensity. From the beginning, the psalmist insists on striking a paradoxical note of hopefulness, talking of strength rather than weakness when we are greeted with the human at the most fragile moment: as an infant, as a child. The human begins her life in weakness: the infant cannot survive on her own but needs care for months before even being able to walk, let alone fend for herself. The dependence and vulnerability of the infant, the constant need for attention, points to how delicate the entire human enterprise is. The continuity of our existence is dependent on this tiny flesh whose only sound is whimper and cry.

The poet revels in this vision and understands it to be an illustration of a key religious paradox: seeming weakness hides ultimate strength. You want to know just how fragile human existence is? Look at a baby, who cannot take care of a single need. Yet, God's glory is glimpsed in the smiles and screams of babies. In fact, when we see a child, we are awed, overcome, happiness breaks out.

Hope lies with the newborn—innocence, purity, sheer potential. Though now defenseless, unable to care for itself, it will eventually prove strong. And this too can be said of the child—what appears weak is closest to the divine and shall inherit the future. Is it not the seemingly powerless infant who holds out the promise of redemption and salvation? We experience the birth of a child, the weak link in the human chain, as unmitigated blessing. Each child is the possible redeemer.[3]

In the portrait of the infant we are presented with the most extreme metaphor of religious belief. In human history that which appears at the moment powerful, ascendant, can be overturned by those who are seemingly weak and out of power. That is the inherent story of Israel—the slave people who defeated the mightiest world power of the time, Egypt. The religious vision is of the triumph of a potential that is hidden now. Religious faith requires imagination, necessitates dreaming and hoping. It enunciates a vision of a hardly believable future. At the moment, power may lie elsewhere than with the righteous, corruption may be the game of the day, but justice will eventually triumph. God may be invisible, but blessing will come. Is the crying, weak, vulnerable child not a miracle beyond imagining? There is a promise of life—a full, blossoming life we can hardly imagine as we stand here holding the infant, the miniature. Hope overrides the fears we may harbor as we feel in our hands the vulnerable present.

Similarly, religious faith necessitates an understanding of the inherent paradoxes of existence. God and God's creation, the world, are one, but in a way that is only disclosed in the future. The religious moment is the moment of birth, when life is full of potential, everything is possible, and yet nothing is tangibly present save hints of what might be. The vision of the cold, rational eye is that nothing else is there but what we see: vulnerability, weakness, human paltriness, the constant accompaniment of our lives—death and decay. Faith, imagination, the world of dreams, overcomes the evidence of the reality that confronts us. Its understandings are deeper, oriented to a future that can only be hinted at now. The psalmist states the paradox baldly:

> From the mouth of infants and sucklings
> You have founded strength against Your besiegers
> quieting enemy and avenger.

3. In traditional Jewish practice, at the time of circumcision or baby naming, an infant is placed on a chair, "the chair of Elijah," since every child may be the one who announces the Messianic age.

What comes out of the mouths of infants and sucklings is an inarticulate cry, yet it is the baby's loud wailing that assures us of a healthy newborn. Is not this primal cry to be heard as the harbinger of salvation? Could this be a metaphor for the position of the supplicant in the temple, who comes with the cry of the heart? Should not that person, weak, defeated, and alone, see herself as reaching towards God in the heavens? (The later Talmudic rabbis were to say that, in our time, all gates of heaven are closed except the gate of tears.)

The phrase "From the mouth . . ." is also evocative of that central human function—speech. This cry of the infant is a harbinger of speech, which will characterize the human being. It is through the power of speech that the human is differentiated from the rest of nature, and it is through the power of speech that God is named in the world. The newborn is more vulnerable than any beast of the field, and yet human consciousness, speech, will give us the power to be triumphant over everything seemingly stronger now. This baby will soon be able to sound God's name in the world.

Here, interestingly, the defeat of the enemy is not described as a pitched battle, not as a war, as, for instance, in the prophetic images of the combat between *Gog* and *Magog* in the end of days, but rather as a "quieting." It is not destruction that is aimed at but rather peace.

The Hebrew word which we've translated as "quieting" is *l'hashbit*, the verbal root of the word "Sabbath." The Sabbath, the day of rest, is the moment of our giving up our instrumental power over the universe and of our finding spiritual succor; is this, then, yet another example of powerlessness exhibiting greater strength than might? Is the author hinting that it is through the Sabbath, that wonderful acknowledgment of our nonmastery of nature, that the enemy, who seems to want to control all, is defeated? Is divine power somehow different from all our conceptions of earthly power, defeating through quietude rather than the noise of battle? And is this God's grandeur: that ultimate peace is attained by different means than conventional armaments?

And yet the image of the baby reminds us of human insufficiency, of our own smallness, our neediness and fragility. The other side of exalting God's power is to be reminded of human paltriness: God is all powerful, the human is vulnerable; God is eternal, the human is condemned to a short life and the ever-present foreboding of death.

> What are human beings that You have been mindful of them,
> the descendants of Adam that You have taken note of them?

In this poem of extreme contrasts and contradictions, and the comparison of heaven and earth with which we began, we have now moved to simultaneously remarking on the blessing of human existence and the realization of our insignificance. Compared with the natural forces arrayed in the heavens, the human is the most transient and the most fragile.

> When I behold Your heavens, the work of Your fingers,
> the moon and stars that You set in place,
>
> what are human beings that You have been mindful of them,
> the descendants of Adam that You have taken note of them?

The human is insignificant in the cosmos, and yet God does care about us. We are descendants of Adam and Eve, God's creations, who were told that they were in formed in God's very likeness, and as such we have enormous power.

Human beings can rule over the rest of nature—everything in the sea, on land, in the air can become subject to human domination. The power of mind, the power of consciousness, the power of human articulation, of culture, of faith and faithfulness makes the human but little lower than the angels. We are weak yet we are strong. We are born inarticulate yet become masters of speech. Even our most fragile and nonverbal moments contain a mysterious ability to manifest strength that only an unseen future will reveal. The paradox is that the fragile human being is the high point of creation. In God's world, weakness is strength, vulnerability the indication of salvation, speech, which has no material existence, is a stronger element than adamantine rock. (Moses is punished because he does not act on the instruction that it is speech which ought to split the rock.) This is a vision that can see salvation in the painful cry of birth; the child, the weakest link in the human story, becomes the source of hope and salvation. To be religious is to see past the obvious, past the surface of existence and to understand that something is at work in the universe which overturns our everyday way of thinking.

The psalmist has explored the paradox of human existence—our mixture of strength and weakness, power and vulnerability. For all that the human is one of the elements in creation, therefore finite, material, mortal, yet the human can exercise power over creation. God's power is pristinely visible in the heavens; the human has been given sway on earth.

> For You have made them little less than divine
> and adorned them with honor and glory;
>
> You have anointed them rulers over Your handiwork,
> laying it all at their feet,
>
> sheep and oxen, all of them,
> along with the animals on the range,
>
> the birds of the heavens, the fish of the sea,
> whatever travels the paths of the seas.

And so we return again to the opening statement

> Adonai—our master—
> How grand is Your name throughout the earth!

What a different meaning this verse has than we first thought! In its first appearance, the verse pointed singlemindedly to God, and the phrase was a simple assertion of God's power. But in the end, we understand the subtleties and paradoxes of power, and God's majesty can seem even more miraculous. The human chorus of worshipers standing in the temple court-yard may experience finitude, fragility—may, in fact, be crying—but in the paradox of religious thinking the seemingly weak have become the symbols of the ultimately victorious. The combination of frailty and almost infinite possibility, of present helplessness and coming maturation, the changing relation time has to all beings, are themes we ponder as God's majesty unfolds.

So the hand of God is subtle and mysterious as well as obvious and ever present. Weakness and strength have quite different meanings in the perspective of time, most especially in the perspective of God's time. Though there are enemies who seem powerful now, hope of a different fu-ture can derive from the slimmest of sources. The cry of the babe echoes in our mind as we speak of God's power. Armies represent only a certain kind of strength. The weak in their faithfulness may have a different and greater strength.

The grandeur of God, which now can only be observed in the distant heavens, will one day be revealed here on earth as well. The hint of that end is in the beginning: human beginning, the cry of the infant, is the fanfare welcoming that approaching time. The human will speak words of praise of God and bring God's kingdom. Earth and heaven will exist in mirrored oneness—in the end of time, as it was at the beginning.[4]

To be religious, says the psalmist, is to embrace the paradoxes of life. To see God's power one must view the world through the glasses of imagination and hope. The affirmation of this imaginative leap is the bringing of God into the world, the uniting of heaven and earth.

4. These very words "in the end as it was at the beginning," are recited as part of the liturgy in the Sephardic version of the doxology.

4

Psalm 91

Who Speaks?

WHEN THE BIBLE SAYS, "In the beginning, God created heaven and earth . . . ," it is an authoritative voice that speaks to us, that tells us about God, describes God's acts, and reports God's speech; the words are spoken by an observer who knows all. Many psalms, too, reflect this stance. As we read a psalm and hear a phrase like "Praise God," we accept the anonymity of its source, for it feels appropriate: it is the same authoritative, all knowing, commanding voice we are used to from so many of our other encounters with the Bible. Who is speaking in these poems? A priest? A Levitical chorus? An Israelite poet? A Judean king? A prophet? The person behind the voice is hidden from us, though we, the readers, may personally experience the message as the collective voice of a tradition or the summoning voice of a traditional authority. As we read, or as we listen, as we enter into the story being told or the poem being recited, we accept the anonymous authority of the text, and allow it to address us.

Another kind of speaking typifies the book of Psalms. The majority of psalms speak with a personal voice, we hear the *I* of the poet, a subjective stance that allows us to visualize a full person, not someone mysteriously hidden behind the anonymous mask of authority. We may be especially engaged by these psalms, for they constitute one of the few places in the Bible where we can encounter a first-person report so consistently. In fact, medieval commentators were so taken aback by this personalization that they attached many of these anonymous, first-person passages to events in David's life. They had difficulty allowing the psalm to exist with the *I* of a common person, but instead returned even this *I* to an authoritative voice: they thought that the only ones who could speak personally were the epic biblical heroes; our own lives were too paltry to reflect upon. But in our generation, the ability to hear such an individual voice expressing personal feelings can be an especially attractive moment in the reading of biblical texts.

What can be even more surprising in the book of Psalms are the moments when the antiphonal voice, the voice responding to the prayer of the psalmist, is the voice of God. Here, God speaks and answers prayer directly. We not only hear our own voice in these psalms, but at these moments are vouchsafed a response. This, after all, is the ultimate wish of prayer: that we might experience an answer—that for a moment we might hear God's direct address to us.

God's speech in Psalms is certainly not oracular, consisting of pronouncements addressed to individuals regarding the future course of their lives; nor does God respond in riddles, or in nonsense syllables that must be unraveled by an interpreter as is the case with the reports of divine speech in ancient Greek literature.[1] Rather, the message is unambiguous and straightforward, reflecting prophetic calls for justice and expressing reassurance to those who act righteously of God's presence and care. The words themselves are frequently quotations or paraphrases and restatements of thoughts and phrases found elsewhere in the Bible, and frequently we can even trace the parallel biblical passage on which the quotation is based.

Drawing on the common faith enunciated by the Prophets, Wisdom literature, or received tradition, these messages from God assert obvious truths of biblical faith. The truths contained in the words spoken by God but written by the psalmist, truths we readily agree with, hide the brazenness of authorial reach. They are believable statements in the mouth of God precisely because they represent essential biblical teaching. Yet, this does not detract from the drama of hearing God speak. The power of God's speech overwhelms all the other voices in these psalms. A person prays and hopes for a response, a contemporary devotee reads the words of the psalm expressing gratitude or perplexity or anguish reflecting inner religious emotions of thankfulness or of torment and then hears the words of God in response and finds reassurance.

---

1. Numbers 12:8 asserts that God's speech to lesser prophets than Moses is of this sort.

Commentators on Psalms have remarked on what they point to as the "performative function" of the recitation of psalms in the temple precincts. Form critics have described rituals, some not mentioned in the Bible, that may have been the occasions on which psalms were recited. They argue that many psalms were intended to evoke the presence of God, to make the listener feel he or she was experiencing an entrance into the divine realm. Such historical reconstructions of the ways in which psalms may have been used in temple times are, of course, speculative.[2] The book of Leviticus, which meticulously describes the sacrificial ritual, never offers any liturgical directions, never describes any words to be recited in approaching the altar; and the psalms themselves do not describe their use in the temple, and so any assertion regarding their ritual use in temple times is purely speculative. One cannot prove or disprove these speculations, and because we lack any evidence, for or against, I rather shy away from these theories. But I think they can shed light on understanding the reaction to psalms in our own day. The recitation of psalms becomes a ritual, one we observe with the hope that it has some effect; in a sense, we "perform" them. What may happen to us through the recitation of psalms is that we hear the verses coming toward us, recited by us but heard in our inner ear, as if spoken by someone else. The recitation may elicit the feeling that we are hearing a voice that speaks across time. When it is God who is the speaker in the psalm, we may come to feel that this is the closest we will get to hearing the voice of God. And even in those psalms that contain no reference to God's speech, in reciting a psalm we hear more than our own speaking. The religious recitation of psalms is an evocative ritual. We ourselves may recite these words, but we are able to hear them as an authoritative voice instructing us, reassuring us, across time.

Placing words in the mouth of God is such an unexpected technique that frequently translators and commentators have failed to notice how easily the psalmist has slipped into this voice. Indeed, sometimes sentences obviously uttered by God are translated as if they are the words of the psalmist, and the dramatic power of the psalm is lost. Ancient Hebrew texts

2. Twentieth-century literary studies of psalms have particularly emphasized this point, most notably Hermann Gunkel (*The Psalms*), who theorized that there was an actual enthronement ceremony. The difficulty is that reconstruction of such a ceremony is purely an imaginative act on the part of the contemporary scholar. A softer version of this position was developed by Herb Levine (*Sing unto God a New Song*), who argues that there need not have been an actual ceremony, but that the ritual and liturgy inspired the imagination of the worshiper.

did not contain any punctuation marks; therefore the quotation marks in translation are always an interpretive addition. Yet there is no doubt that many psalms contain direct quotation of divine speech, and when we pay attention to who the speaker is, we recover the literary power of those psalms. Such moments can become ones in which words have the power to evoke God's presence.

Frequently a particular psalm speaks not with a single voice, but as we read closely, we can detect multiple voices. Sometimes we experience a leader calling and a chorus responding—the two voices creating a rhythmic antiphonal dialogue. At other times quite a different drama plays itself out: we may hear the psalmist speaking personally, and then another voice (perhaps a priest or a Levitical chorus) responds, as if in answer to the plea of the devotee. At times we may feel that the multiple voices expressed in a psalm represent the multiple voices we hear inside our own hearts. Our own subjective arguments become contending voices in the psalm. It is this play of voices that allows the psalmist to enunciate yet another voice: to allow us to hear the voice of God affirming that our prayers are heard.

Perhaps it was the setting of at least some psalms that encouraged this literary device: greeted with songs sung by the choir, the devotee entering the temple precincts felt a closeness to God available nowhere else. He or she may have made this pilgrimage to give thanks, pray for help, atone for some act whose guilt was especially pressing, or come to the temple to hear God's instruction. That heightened expectation allowed for a poetic voice of God responding to the devotee. The temple, after all, was supposed to guarantee the presence of God. So, if psalms were indeed sung by the Levites or a temple choir, then we could well imagine that the literary device of the quotation of God took on an almost personified expression in the setting of the temple, evoking the very presence of God in response to the devotee's prayers. I rather think that it was not the temple itself that was the setting for these words—the ritual itself contained enough power that it needed no additional comment—but rather it was the looking toward the temple, the expectation of what would occur there, that aroused the imaginative power of these psalmists. Thus, these may be pilgrims' poems, composed and recited on the journey to the temple. The intense expectation may have given rise to the need to hear God's voice directly, to anticipate meeting God in the temple, to imagine what it must be like to be there.

But we need not enter into historical speculation to appreciate the literary innovation of these psalms. In allowing us to hear God's response to our prayers, the psalmist takes us to a realm normally foreclosed to us. At times of prayer, it is a world we wish and hope for, and these psalms take an imaginative leap we all secretly desire. It should be added that having moved to the realm of imagination in describing God's own speaking, it is not surprising that some of these psalms are filled with fantasy and illusion, or that the scene that is set by the poem is entirely one of fantasy. Indeed, if these are pilgrim psalms, the entire poem is a vast imagining.

In this chapter and the next, I will illustrate these points through two very different psalms in which the speech of God becomes a critical element in the development of the poem.

PSALM 91

1   Whoever dwells in the secret places of the One on high
lodges in the shadow of the Almighty.

2   I would say to Adonai, "My refuge, my tower,
my God." I would trust Him.[3]

3   For He will save you from the fowler's trap,
from destructive plague;

4   With His pinions He will cover you;
beneath His wings you will find refuge;

His faithfulness are armor and shields.

5   You will not fear the terror of the night,
the flight of an arrow by daylight,

6   the plague stalking in the dark,
or the scourge that may ravage at noon.

7   A thousand may fall to your left,
ten thousand to your right,
but nothing shall reach you.

8   For you have but to look with your eyes,
and you shall see the recompense of the wicked.

9   "For You, Adonai, are my protection."

You have made your refuge the One on high—

---

3. Once again, I apologize to readers for the heavily gendered language of the translation, but I found no other way to convey the third-person yet personal quality of the opening stanzas and the contrasting first-person statement of God at the end.

10   no harm will befall you,
       no disease touch your tent.

11   For He will order His angels for you,
       to guard you wherever you go.

12   They will carry you in their hands
       lest you stub your toe on a rock.

13   You will tread on cubs and vipers;
       trample on lions and asps.

14   "Because he desired Me, I will rescue him;
       I will raise him up, for he knows My name.

15   When he calls on Me, I will answer him;
       I will be with him in distress;
       I will strengthen him, honor him;

16   I will sate him with a full life,
       and show him My salvation."[4]

This is a psalm offering reassurance, safety for the pilgrim. Its power is due in part to the multiple voices we hear. In the very first three sentences of this psalm we meet three distinct speakers and the intertwining of these voices prepares us for the emergence of yet another voice at the end of the poem: the voice of God. Who speaks the very first sentence?

> Whoever dwells in the secret places of the One on high
> lodges in the shadow of the Almighty.

This opening line is an almost anonymous heading appropriate to all that follows, as if the poem had a title. The words may be those of an adage, a reassuring statement of faith, a prayer, a quotation. We might hear it as the opening statement of the priest as the pilgrim enters the temple, or see it as a sign over the entranceway remarking on the life of faith. Or perhaps it is the musing of the poet, thinking about the reasons to remain faithful. It may be the voice of a chorus or speaker instructing the devotee in the life of the godly, followed by the disciple then announcing his acquiescence in the second sentence. Or perhaps, were there punctuation marks in biblical times, the sentence might have been followed by three dots. It is the

---

4. Or "and display him in my victory march," meaning allow him to march with me in victory.

anonymous voice of faith on which the rest of the psalm is a meditation and response.

There is an elusiveness to this opening thought, with its mention of the secret places, and its suggestive but difficult reference to dwelling on high—after all, while alive, humans can sleep in heaven only metaphorically.

Where is this hidden place? What does it mean to live in the shadow of God? If God is on high, how does one reach God? This first sentence uses neither the personal nor the generic name of God, instead we meet a distant and almost anonymous Almighty (Hebrew: *shaddai*). This lack of designation matches the allusion to the "secret places," and is picked up further with the thought that we are in the "shadow" of the Almighty—shadows are only hints of real figures—important descriptive features are missing. Almost every allusion in this first sentence hides as much as it reveals. The adage poses as many questions as it seeks to answer, and seemingly the psalm itself unfolds the meaning of the opening phrases.

The speaker of the second verse is clearly distinguished from the voice articulated in the first. The insertion of the personal *I* changes the effect of the opening line even if it is a repetition of its central idea. It is perhaps a response:

> I would say to Adonai, "My refuge, my tower,
> my God." I would trust Him.

I am to be counted among the faithful, announces the pilgrim. Implied is that the devotee wants to be counted among those who "dwell" with God, those who are protected by God. But the devotee has also changed the terms in which devotion is cast. In the mouth of the devotee, the secret places are now described as a fort, a protected tower, a visibly secured place, and God is referred to with both the personal and generic name of divinity.

A new voice introduces yet another metaphor of God's protection, depicting God as a bird guarding its young. The devotee is nestled, hidden, in God's wings, and is carried through the sky, on high, soaring over whatever dangers life presents. The author of verses 3 to 8 addresses the pilgrim directly; the speech is not phrased in the third person but in the second person: "you." We might imagine this speaker as the priest or elder, the instructor in the life of faith. It may be the same speaker who opened the psalm in an anonymous third-person voice, now addressing the pilgrim directly. What is different is that there is a conversation: the pilgrim and the "elder" are addressing each other: the *I* of the psalmist, the declaration of faith, has brought the direct response of the leader.

(It is possible to see the poem in more imaginative terms: we may find both voices to be that of the poet, and perhaps what is taking place here is an internal dialogue in which the author unifies his soul through the articulation of diverse voices: the first touching on his fears, the second sounding words of reassurance. Thus the voices become a medley of our own inner voices.)

The duality of voice is echoed in verse 9, when once again we hear the devotee speaking personally in response to the reassuring words that have punctuated the intervening verses:

> "For You, Adonai, are my protection."

Thus, the conversation continues, and this first-person affirmation is again followed by the leader's return, addressing the pilgrim directly in the second person:

> You have made your refuge the One on high—
> no harm will befall you . . .

The second intonation of blessing, from verses 10 to 13, repeats the assurances offered in the first, stating them in only slightly different manner. The first blessing (verses 3–8) talks of God carrying the penitent in His arms, while in the second an angelic courier safeguards the devotee. In the first part it is the human who is frequently the enemy, hunting other humans like an animal, and it is a bird that saves the human; in the second it is the animal world that is the enemy attacking the human. In the first, the pilgrim flies through the air; in the second part, the pilgrim is on the road, protected in his travels. In both sections, the images of danger are quite similar—protection from plague and attack. Thus the second half of the poem echoes the first, though with a lessening of both the care and the threat. The two parts, for all their differences, are elaborations of similar themes.

These two stanzas are separated, as we have said, by the assertion of faithfulness by the devotee in verse 9. The use of this particular device to divide the two halves is critical—the multiple voices introduced at the beginning of the psalm are reemphasized by the divide in the middle and will prepare us for the entrance of the third voice, that of God, who, from verse 14 to the end, responds to the affirmation of the pious.

But this description misses an important point: the way fantasy and imagination have overtaken us. In the first part of the poem, God is described as a bird, carrying the poet by her pinions, nestling the psalmist in her wings. In the second description, it is the poet who has become birdlike, skipping over vipers' nests, seemingly flying above all the traps of the earth.

The power of faith and belief has allowed the devotee to enter into a world of imagination and fantasy, of transformed reality. It is a "flight of fancy." And as in surrealistic dreams, the dangers are drawn concretely and graphically: the hunter's trap, the viper's nest, and the instruments of escape and protection, flying above it all, a kind of magic carpet, are images common to fantasy life.

In this dream-like fantasy, a mere glance will show how evil is punished:

> For you have but to look with your eyes,
> and you shall see the recompense of the wicked.

Unlike the everyday reality we meet in which it is not obvious that transgressors are punished, in this vision the pilgrim has but to look about and the punishment of the evildoers will be obvious.

It will be amid this world of fantasy and imagination that God's speech will unfold. The last three verses (14–16) consist of God's own affirmation of the message of safety and protection. The promise of the priest or of the chorus that the pilgrim will be sheltered and unharmed, which has been the substance of their two speeches, now receives its confirmation in the voice of God. Verses 14, 15, and 16 are filled with verbs of assurance, phrased in the first person: "I will save him," "I will raise him up," "I will answer him," "I will strengthen him," "I will honor him," "I will sate him," "I will show him." In Hebrew, each of these phrases is contracted into one word; the effect is to sum up what had been promised and give a divine imprimatur, an absolute assurance of protection. What can be more comforting than the very voice of God vouchsafing the promise of safety and security? This cascade of verbs adds up to God's total agreement, an unqualified assurance.

> "Because he desired Me, I will rescue him;
> I will raise him up, for he knows My name.
>
> When he calls on Me, I will answer him;
> I will be with him in distress;
> I will strengthen him, honor him;"

The divine pledge serves as validation of the promises offered earlier in the poem. What is offered is an absolute validation of God's constant care and supreme assurance of safety, an affirmation by God that the faith that has been described by the priest or elder is true. The verbs assuring protection and safe keeping, of being raised up and strengthened, are appropriate to the images elaborated in the earlier stanzas which remarked on the danger roundabout.

But something new happens in God's speech and is enunciated in the culmination, the final verse, verse 16.

> I will sate him with a full life,
> and show him My salvation.

Earlier God's reward was couched in terms of shielding the righteous from enemies: the metaphors were of war, battle, and victory, the expressed hope was of defeat of evil. But now when God climaxes God's own speech, God promises something that had not been mentioned or even alluded to earlier: the fullness of days, time. It is the fullness of life that is the ultimate reward. The images of protection voiced earlier were of salvation from the negative—saving from harm. Only God's voice is able to assure the positive: length of days, peacefulness, and bounty. And the life of the pilgrim is tied to something greater: God's triumph. The pilgrim himself, proudly living and breathing, will be an outward sign of God's presence and power.

Had the poem only contained the reassurance of the priestly voice, it would have been merely a pious recitation of received beliefs. Readers would have been left with the awareness of danger and the promise of divine protection, but it would have had the air of stock piety. By having God speak words of assurance, the simple statement of faith with which the psalm began has been granted a grandeur it would not otherwise have had. The poem gains its power through the progression of a dialogue that is then capped by God's own hopeful words. And the voice of God takes us to a place only God can reassure us about—the future. This is an ultimate imaginative act on the part of the devotee, for the future has no reality, it only exists as an act of consciousness. In imagining that future, the psalmist offers the ultimate reassurance of prayer: the future contains hope, blessing will come.

The future that is promised is not only that of individual salvation. The last line ("... and show him my salvation") alludes to a time of ultimacy for the world, when God and the world will be one, when the individual will not only be protected but when all will recognize God's presence. This time, which is unknown to us, is truly the secret of the One on high, but in the knowledge that that time must come lies the hope of ultimate protection on which the pilgrim depends.

Many psalms express doubt. In many psalms there is a plea for help. The stated purpose of these psalms is that we voice our innermost need, hoping to be heard and wishing for a response. In Psalm 91, where we actually hear God speak, we cross over beyond a world of hope to the actualization of imagination—we move beyond the silence which normally greets us in prayer. This may be the function of all psalms: through our speaking, through voicing our innermost reality of hope and fear, longing and belief alongside words of reassurance given to us by a tradition of faith, a greater reality opens up to us and our own pain is put in perspective. Ritual and prayer may allow us to grasp that which can never be seen, only sometimes imagined, imagined through the power of words—the beyond that summons us. The words allow us to see and hear what is otherwise foreclosed to us: a hearing of the yes of divine response and reassurance. The psalmist tells this tale with the realization that it can only be told when we enter the poetic world, when language takes flight.

5

Psalm 82

Justice

GOD IS THE GUARANTOR of justice; that is the sine quo non of biblical religion. While appeals to justice and themes of justice may also be found throughout the ancient world, only in Israel could it be said: "love the stranger as yourself, for you were once strangers in the land of Egypt; I, Adonai, am your God" (Leviticus 19:34). The Greeks could talk of gods at war and could think of humans, victims of their endless rivalry, as suffering an accidental fate; the Babylonians could picture human beings as serfs of the gods and understand the contemporary social hierarchy as the inherent order of creation; the Egyptians could see all of life as a preparation for another world that would eternally reflect the ideal imagined on earth, a realm of slaves and masters; but Israel saw the exodus as central to its faith, which meant that the single most important characteristic of God was that God was liberator, God was protector of the least secure elements of society: the stranger, the orphan and the widow. Israelite religion understood that the central religious drama was enacted in the relationship of society to justice, here and now. The insight of the author of the first chapter of Genesis—that creation is God's gift, that the human is the apex of creation, and that each of us reflects God's very image—ultimately is a call for each of us to recognize the image of God in the other. Thus Abraham could speak to God and ask, "Should not the judge of all the earth act justly?" (Genesis 18:25). The triumph of monotheism in Israel meant that God was singly responsible for a just order in the universe.

Nowhere is this understanding that justice is the central yardstick of redemption more ingeniously displayed than in Psalm 82. In a brazen imaginative leap, we are admitted as spectators to the heavenly court where divine judgment is being rendered. We see a trial in progress; the accused are the divine representatives of human beings. We are allowed to hear God's direct speech enunciating the ultimate test of divinity: the establishment of justice on earth. And yet by the end, God's own words, though expressing reassurance, are almost turned into a challenge to God.

The psalm is entirely made up of alternating voices, stage cues voiced by the psalmist followed by God's own speech. The alternation of voice creates drama, a veritable fantasy fashioned from biblical theology. We are in the world of theatrical illusion, but since the assumptions of the poem are so fundamental to biblical religion, it all becomes a believable tale. This entry into God's court takes us out of, as it were, the realm of psalmody, of prayer, into a world of theater, and it is only as we reach the end that we are returned to the human realm and therefore to the world of petition.

PSALM 82

1   A song of Asaf:
God stands in the divine assembly;
among the divine beings God pronounces judgment.

2   "How long will you judge perversely,
showing favor to the wicked?" *Selah*

3   "Take up the case of the wretched and the orphan,
vindicate the lowly and the poor,

4   rescue the wretched and the needy;
save them from the hand of the wicked."

5   They do not comprehend or understand,
they go about in darkness;
all the foundations of earth totter.

6   "I had once said that you were divine beings,
children of the Most High, all of you;

7   but you shall die as humans do,
fall like any prince."

8   Arise, O God, judge the earth,
for all the nations are Your possession.

The first line of the psalm sets the scene for the drama that is about to unfold.

> God stands in the divine assembly;
> among the divine beings God pronounces judgment.

The poem has become a script and we seemingly are party to a stage direction. Indeed the power of the line rests in the disappearance of the poet; the line is recited in an anonymous third person voice announcing what is occurring in the heavens. This is a voice which will return twice in the psalm: once in verse 5 before the pronouncement of judgment, where it still carries its anonymous ring, and then again at the end in verse 8, when it becomes prayerful—at which point the poem moves from theater to temple, from heaven back to earth. Until that last line, any affective statement on the part of the supplicant is absent, as well as any personalization. The emotional display in the midst of the poem is left to God. The line is effective precisely because it is deadpan.

As we have said, the poem transports us out of our own earthly reality and invites us to watch a scene taking place in heaven. If this poem was in fact written for recitation in the temple precincts, we can imagine it taking on enormous power for the devotee, who having ascended the pilgrim stairs leading to the temple mount, and believing that he or she is as close to God as one can come on earth, now looks heavenward and imagines the skies opening up and the heavenly court being revealed. This is quite literally theater, the audience having entered a controlled space; stage center, the words of the play are declaimed. The poem is a daring act of imagination, made believable through ritual.

As is so often the case with modern stage directions, we are not only given a bare-bones description of the arrangement of the set and the characters onstage, but the directions are critical in telling us something about the action about to be displayed. God is standing in the court—in the ancient world, the judge stands when judgment is about to be delivered. We know therefore that this is a formal judicial proceeding and guilt or innocence is about to be pronounced.[1]

At first, the poem is vague about who the defendants are. God is standing amid the "assembly of divine beings," and suddenly we realize it is they who are on trial—the semigodly forces of the universe that have been responsible for the daily activity of life—the lesser gods who rule us. (By the

---

1. Sarna, *On the Book of Psalms.*

end of the poem they will be expelled from the heavenly court—they are no longer divine and now will die.)[2]

> "How long will you judge perversely,
> showing favor to the wicked?" *Selah*
>
> "Take up the case of the wretched and the orphan,
> vindicate the lowly and the poor,
>
> rescue the wretched and the needy;
> save them from the hand of the wicked."

If we were indeed to hear God speak, these are the words that we would expect to hear. It is the biblical teaching endlessly reiterated by the prophets: society is to be judged by its treatment of the disenfranchised, the weakest elements; God is the guarantor of the rights of the powerless. The prayers and the voices of the oppressed will be heard in heaven even as their rights are ignored here on earth—ultimately God will judge the powerful who lord it over them now. The words are simple, unadorned, in the biblical mind, the most basic formula.

Now the psalmist speaks again. The author has moved from giving pure stage directions to become a narrator and commentator. This voice describes the inner state of the heavenly beings who are being judged.

> They do not comprehend or understand,
> they go about in darkness;
> all the foundations of earth totter.

It is clear that this verse is spoken by someone other than God, the author of the previous two verses, because the heavenly beings are addressed in the third person; when God speaks, they are addressed directly in the second person. Yet because the narrator has now shifted his commentary from simply setting the stage, as he does in the opening verse, to describing the inner state of the characters, the fact that this is no longer the speech of God is frequently missed. Thus many translations continue quotation marks around this sentence as if it simply were a continuation of God's speech.[3]

2. There are repeated references to "fallen angels" in the Bible, most notably the *n'filim* in Genesis 6:4.

3. The New English Bible (NEB) translation simply changes "they" to "you," totally vitiating the grammatical problem: "But you know nothing, you understand nothing . . ." Sarna, *On the Book of Psalms*, 174, refuses to take a position on whether it is God speaking or the psalmist. The Jewish medieval commentator Ibn Ezra, sensitive to the

Trust Buber, the biblical scholar and philosopher, the "master of dialogue," to be sensitive to the variety of voices and to understand how this
psalm is constructed out of the movement of speech between God, who is
passing judgment in the heavenly court, and the psalmist commenting on
earth. Martin Buber writes:

> The deeper my experience of life, the more thoroughly do I un-
> derstand this Psalm, which is so variously interpreted and yet in
> the end is so simple . . .The structure is determined by the fact that
> the Psalm, unlike most, does not express an emotion but presents
> a visionary event. In the midst of this event are two speeches of
> God, uttered at two different stages of the event. These speeches
> are enclosed within three sayings of the Psalmist. The first say-
> ing tells us about the circumstances of the event, the second leads
> from the first to the second stage of the event, while the third, with
> which the Psalmist concludes, leaves the event which has been
> contemplated, and, as it were, inferring from it, calls directly upon
> the God who has been at work on it.[4]

God's opening speech is the reading of the indictment by which the defendants will be judged. The psalmist acts almost as a court reporter, telling us of the guilt of the defendants. Not only have they not led the world
to justice, but they are guilty in their very beings because they have no
regret. They can never admit their guilt, because they have no comprehen-
sion of how fundamental their sin is. They had one basic function: to bring
justice to the world; instead they frittered away their energy, perhaps on
themselves, perhaps in promoting corruption. We are not told what they
were doing, but this we do know—the world does not reflect the work of
justice which they were charged to bring into being. Further, the court has
found that the defendants themselves are so steeped in injustice that they
no longer know what justice looks like—"They do not understand." They
understand divinity and social hierarchy to be about the exercise of power
not the creation of a just society. Their corruption is total, they lack a fundamental understanding of their role, which makes the sentence which God
then pronounces fully appropriate.

Presumably the congregation hearing the psalm could empathize
immediately with the reality evoked by these lines. The world which they

---

grammatical change, specifically notes that this verse is spoken by the psalmist and is no
longer the speech of God.

4. Buber, *Good and Evil*, 20.

inhabited was unjust. But it is not only a human concern; we are told that "the very foundations of the earth are shaken." The injustice being committed undoes creation. It has the strength to turn back the world to the chaos out of which it emanated. It is the power of God, the meaning of creation, which is ultimately threatened by the conditions prevalent on earth. God's demotion of the heavenly beings, God's insistence that they die like humans and cease to have the power of gods, is a restoration of the rightful meaning of creation.

> "I had once said that you were divine beings,
> children of the Most High, all of you;
>
> but you shall die as humans do,
> fall like any prince."

The rightful order in heaven, the proper sense of creation, ought to lead to the proper order here on earth. This is now emphasized by the way in which these supposed "divine beings," these supposed "children of God," are sentenced to die as humans do, are banished from the heavenly stage. God has no rival for power, therefore the world is ordered: justice ought to reign. As Abraham says to God, "Will the judge of all the earth not deal justly?" (Genesis 18:25). And so the psalmist can pray that heaven and earth might meet:

> Arise, O God, judge the earth,
> for all the nations are Your possession.

In the end, the psalmist discards the role of the stage director and enters as a character on stage. The poet's words which are the last to be spoken transform the character of the whole psalm. It is not only a glimpse into heaven, it is a prayer. The scene in heaven has been a believable evocation establishing God as singly responsible for the rule of earth; any lesser beings have been deposed because of their corruption. The sole yardstick, God's justice, has been firmly established as the proper measuring rod for governance. That is the heart of the biblical message.

But the reality we meet is not that of a just world. In fact God, with infinite vision, has passed that very judgment; God has vouchsafed that justice does not currently rule this world. The corruption of the world is a case proven in heaven. Now that God is responsible for the world, ought not justice to reign?

At the heart of the poem there is a call to God. The psalm contains an implicit indictment of God, which the drama has cloaked until now behind the indictment of the lesser divine beings. If God indeed rules the earth, why is not justice the order of the day?

The appeal for God to "rise" is to be understood in the technical meaning of the term used in the beginning of the psalm. God's rising would constitute the giving of judgment, the assumption of ultimate authority. Will the moment of heavenly judgment now move on to judgment of the earth? Will we see the consequence of God's rule here on earth? For all that the poem has offered us reassurance, it has also opened a fissure that is an implicit argument with God. God rules supremely in the world, but that assertion also leads to the question: why is that not visible on earth? Cannot a new court scene be established, one which will portend an age of justice here on earth? Cannot the vision of a heavenly order pervade the earth?

That we can see God operating justly in heaven carries with it a notable assurance. This vision counters any sense of the absence of God. Yet, the appeal to God to institute justice reflects the knowledge of the psalmist that the triumph of evil represents the absence of divine intervention, the disappearance of God. The psalmist, who has enunciated God's speech, addresses us in a world seemingly experiencing God's silence. And so, the psalm ends with a plea.

Most psalms, of course, do not include or end with God's speaking; on the contrary, their opposite is much more prevalent in psalms, the sense of waiting for God, the feeling of God's absence. "Do not delay" is the plaint of so many psalms. But almost all psalms set up the expectancy of the response of God, the entrance of God onto the stage of history, the affirming presence of God. When we read psalms, that expectancy, joined as it is with the voice of tradition, grows so strong that we can almost experience ourselves coming into the presence of God. It is the magic of some psalms to have given voice to that expectancy and to have created the dramatic means for viewing and hearing the unseen God who is ever present. We live with the silence of God, yet through the language of psalms, in the poetry of prayer, we evoke God's presence and the voice of response. An act of imagination overcomes the abyss of silence. Psalm 82 is masterful in taking us to the limits of faith, in displaying the inner workings of heaven, in showing us the triumph of justice on high. Yet, because we are east of Eden, because we deal with earthly realities, the rift between the heavenly ideal and our everyday experience remains poignant. Ultimately, we are left with our faces turned heavenward. The last lines of the poem are both an argument with God and a prayer for the intervention of the divine. As in Abraham's plea in the dialogue with God before the destruction of Sodom and Gomorrah, "Would not the judge of all the earth act justly?" God has expelled the unjust from heaven. There are now no divine forces aiding cruelty and injustice. Is this then not the moment when God shall rule justly over all the world?

At the end of the poem, expectantly, we look heavenward with a plea and with a question.

6

Psalm 23

God's Care

THE SETTING OF PSALM 82 is heaven, but the setting of Psalm 23 is here on earth and generations of readers have seen in Psalm 23 the ultimate expression of God's care. In times of crisis—when suffering illness, experiencing tragedy or facing death—supplicants have turned to Psalm 23 for comfort. If we are to understand the theological norm of biblical religion, Psalm 23 offers us one of the most beautiful expressions of God's involvement with our everyday life. It affirms God's presence in our lives and promises even further, deeper love and care in the future.

The psalm moves from very concrete images of the day-to-day world to visions of Edenic fulfillment, from satisfaction of the simplest needs to visions of overabundance. Its mixture of dream-like fantasy and concrete reality leads to an ultimate vision of a fulfilled life. Perhaps it is precisely this, the graceful leap from reality to an imagined future that has made this psalm so appealing to the generations. The poem was not originally a vision of the afterlife—there is no allusion to a life hereafter in the poem itself—but an expression of faith in God's care in the here and now and a vision of the wonders that may be provided the person of faith. Though it has become associated with funerals and death, it is an expression of the possibility of the fullness of life.

At first glance the literary structure seems quite simple, but as we look closer we will be struck by some of its complexity. The poem contains two parts, each elaborating a different metaphor. First we meet the image of the shepherd tending the flock, then we are invited into God's house. Thus the poem contains two stanzas, built around two distinct metaphors. Psalms may contain three, sometimes four stanzas, but in their simplest form psalms may have only two, the second one elaborating and extending the image developed in the first.[1] This type of two-stanza psalm most clearly replicates the aesthetics of the simple biblical poetic sentence where the second clause develops the idea of the first part in a way that deepens the idea.

The two metaphors of the poem elaborate God's care. There is no transition between the two, but they are sufficiently different images that readers can easily see that the poem has two distinct parts. The opening stanza spells out the theme of God as shepherd tending the flock, the pious as sheep. This is followed by a shift in which the devotee is pictured as a perfectly sated guest in God's house. The second stanza of Psalm 23, though building on the themes of the initial image, takes us considerably beyond where the first part left us. We go from outdoors to indoors, from earthly peace to heavenly peace, from normal sequential time of day and night to never-ending eternal time, from adequate provisioning to overflowing abundance. The movement from the first image to the second gives the poem its energy.

PSALM 23

A Davidic Psalm:

1   Adonai is my shepherd;
     I will not lack.

2   He will lay me down in green pastures
     lead me to still waters,
     renew my life,

3   guide me in right paths
     for the sake of His own name.

---

1. Some psalms, though, do not break neatly into stanzas but rather are governed by a different poetic sensibility, most notably the acrostic psalms, those that play on the letters of the Hebrew alphabet. These psalms have a different organizing principle: each line has significance on its own, and there is no development or progression in the psalm—some commentators have found that these break into sections with common themes. Similarly, the fifteen Songs of Ascent represent a different poetic form. In general, though, readers are well served in trying to locate the stanzas of a psalm, for the structure offers an important key needed to unlock meaning.

4   Even if I were to walk through a valley as dark as death,
     I would fear no wrong
     for You are with me;
     Your rod and Your staff,
     they would comfort me.

5   You would spread a table for me in full view of my besiegers;
     anoint my head with oil;
     my cup overflowing.

6   Only goodness and steadfast love shall pursue me all the days of my
     life,
     and I shall dwell in the house of Adonai
     till the end of time.

The poem expresses a feeling of remarkable closeness to God. God's personal name is mentioned in the first and last verses, forming a frame for the poem. Although the middle sections use only pronouns for God—most of the poem refers to God in the third person—the second person, "You," is employed in the verse at the very center of the poem: "For You are with me . . ." This is in fact the whole point of the psalm—the blessings of my life are there because God is with me in a very personal way.

The first four verses of the poem speak of the good shepherd in an extended metaphor for God's care. The shepherd leads his flock through dangerous circumstance yet minds each of his sheep, providing them with a place of pasture, soft grass to lie down on, water to quench their thirst. These opening verses are pastoral images of peace and contentment and serve to interpret the opening line: since God is my shepherd, I lack nothing. The images enunciated here deal with the most basic elements of nurture and care: adequate diet, water, rest for the weary. If you will, these are the bodily concerns of the human, our animal needs, and it is fitting that they are described through the image of the shepherd caring for sheep.

Though these are purely physical images, there are hints of the spiritual even here. Thus the waters are still, restful, peaceful, and the paths are straight, right (implying righteous). A meeting of the physical and spiritual is represented by the phrase "for the sake of His own name," for the biblical use of God's name refers exclusively to the meeting of heaven and earth, the acknowledgment of heavenly blessing and promise in earthly reality.

This pastoral scene is broken into with the mention of a dark valley, or, as in the classic translations, the valley of the shadow of death. For the first time an image of danger enters the poem. As the modern commentator

Zvi Adar has noted, "The emotions we experience facing the 'valley of darkness' stand in total opposition to that of being led to the 'still waters.'"[2]

But even here, facing the utmost danger—the threat of the unknown, the terrible darkness looming over the sheep who might slip and fall over a precipice—we are assured of God's presence. The poet expresses confidence that there is no real reason to fear so long as God is the protector.

> Your rod and Your staff,
> they would comfort me

The shepherd walks with her staff, the top part is hooked, pulling wayward sheep toward her, the bottom part is a straight stick, pushing sheep who are not moving forward fast enough. There is an allusion here of the buffeting of life, the pushing and pulling of everyday existence, which might be a source of despair, and yet that the poet understands as part of God's instruction. The ups and downs of life suffered and survived by the ones in God's care are an indication of God's accompanying presence and support. Note that during this buffeting, the sheep are led on "the right path." The Hebrew, even more than the English, contains the overtone of right as righteousness, that is, that the right paths are moral paths, just paths. Again, we have a hint here of what will become explicit at the end of the poem, that the nurture described is not simply physical but spiritual. But whether physical or spiritual is meant, the outcome is clear: God cares for us well.

Without any transition, the second metaphor now begins. In this psalm one stanza flows so gracefully to the next that we hardly notice where one stanza ends and the other begins. And in this second image the supplicant is no longer a sheep lying in the field but a human being sitting at a table, and God has created the perfect house as shelter. Here there is not only adequate care, there is an overflowing of goodness. Not only is there food, but the cup, probably the winecup, now runs over. Similarly, not only is there a decent place to lie down, but the devotee can now luxuriate, as if at a spa—the poet is anointed with soothing oil.

The last verse of the shepherd image, verse 4, contains the hint of danger, the valley which threatens the sheep, and the first verse of the vision of the guest in the house, verse 5, mentions the enemies over against whom the table is set. This reference to threat constitutes the connecting link between the two metaphors of the two stanzas, and makes us less conscious of the transition. It also assures a mirrored arrangement so that the first

2. Adar, *The Book of Psalms*, 142.

stanza moves from pacific waters to the threat of danger, while the second goes from danger to completely sheltering peace, and it will be on that note that the poem will conclude. The outside world through which the flock roams may have contained physical threats from which the sheep needed to be protected, but having been brought inside God's house the devotee will achieve absolute security. Enemies are locked out, left peering through the window, jealous of God's servant. Life is filled with danger, but God will offer appropriate protection.

But it is not only that the devotee will be safe, protected by God's care. This second metaphor goes beyond the sustenance of daily life, to the fullness of blessing in an Edenic time and place, and as we reach the end of the poem we discover evil is banished, there are no dark forces in pursuit, there is no longer even the hint of a dangerous threat for only goodness and mercy pursue the devotee all the days of life. The outside world may have been a source of the unexpected and the dangerous, but now the poet sits in God's house, in an enclosed space, fully shielded. Outside one may have been subject to misstep (there is always an abyss at the side of the mountain), here no danger can lurk. In the scene depicted in the first stanza, we might have hoped for a good night's sleep, a place to lie down and feel protected, but what we received now instead is a cornucopia of wonderful blessings and gifts.

This image of God's house may be a reference to the temple, but the image contained here is more than that—it is of some idealized temple, perhaps the heavenly temple of which the earthly one is but a reflection. The recorded biblical procedure is that only the priests ate in the temple precincts itself, but here the psalmist is sitting at God's table, satiating himself. Rather than the human having set the table of shewbread for the deity in the inner chamber, as the Bible prescribes for the sanctuary ritual, God has set the table for the human guest. The meal is not a sacrifice to God, but rather God's welcoming bounty to God's guests. The idealized temple is like an idealized earth, an Edenic place, in which God is the priest and the human's needs are served. Creation has been fulfilled—the earthly has become heavenly.

We have noted that the movement from the first metaphor of the sheep in the field to the second of the guest in God's house is a movement from outside inward. Inwardness is the residence of spirituality, and in fact by the end, the poet describes the blessing and abundance God offers in purely spiritual terms:

> Only goodness and steadfast love shall pursue me all the days of my life,
> and I shall dwell in the house of Adonai
> till the end of time.

Goodness and steadfast love are qualities of relationship. They describe both the feelings that motivate actions and the actions themselves. They are the intangibles for which we yearn from the other. To live in a world of goodness and steadfast love is to have one's dreams of an ideal world fulfilled. And more, this movement from the realistic image of the shepherd to the ideal being enunciated here is completed at the end of the poem where the greatest blessing that God can bestow is that which is invisible and yet that which is necessary for existence: time.

The Hebrew of the last line translates as "the length of days," and surely one meaning of that phrase in Psalms is the fullness of life, that is to say, a long life. In this interpretation, the psalmist imagines living out the rest of his life in God's house. (Similarly, Psalm 92 talks of being planted in God's house, "all the days of my life.") But the "length of days" also carries with it another connotation, not only longevity but literally the fullness of time, eternity. In another psalm that connection is made explicit: "the length of days, which is forever" (Psalm 21:4). The spiritual wish has burst the bonds of all concrete reality; God's nurture will burst all boundaries in an overflowing bounty, endless time. To be in God's care is to inherit eternity. Certainly, that is the way this poem has been read through the generations.

The issue of time is not incidental to the poem. There is an intentional ambiguity in the use of time throughout the poem.[3] Translators have struggled over whether to render the verbs of this psalm in the future tense or in the present tense. In biblical Hebrew, the past tense indicates action already performed, and the future indicates action not yet completed—the continuous present. The old King James Version tried to preserve some appreciation of this ambiguity, so those editors translated the first sentence as a future tense and the rest in the present tense, capturing in some measure a sense of the future made present:

> The Lord is my shepherd,
> I shall not want.
> He maketh me to lie down in green pastures;
> he leadeth me beside the still waters . . .

with the subsequent verses continuing the present tense.

3. For an extended discussion of the use of time in Psalms, see chapter 8, below.

The new JPS translation takes a different route translating it all in the present tense:

> The Lord is my shepherd,
> I lack nothing.
> He makes me lie down in green pastures;
> He leads me to water in places of repose . . .

Others translate it entirely in the future tense:

> God is my shepherd
> I shall not want.
> He will bring me into meadows of young grass,
> he will guide me beside quiet water . . .[4]

I have chosen to translate the text consistently in the future so that readers realize that there is no change of tense in the Hebrew verbs themselves. What we are experiencing in the poem is a future made present, a hope felt so strongly that it can almost be experienced in the now, though certainly I would think that all the translators, even those who translate the poem in the present, would agree that the poet is not experiencing these conditions in reality, for the metaphors are too hyperbolic for that, and it is clear that the last line of the poem is an expression of hope, of an ideal, not of reality. Thus the poem is a making present through prayer, a statement of faith that is so strong that the hope is experienced as reality and the gift of the poet is to allow us, the readers, to sense God's presence becoming present, now. This is an ultimate act of faith, turning hope into a perceived present.

One of the central functions of the temple is to allow the supplicant to feel refreshed, renewed, sins having been wiped away, no more trouble is to be anticipated. This has happened in this poem, but the renewal has led us to unexpected places, to a fullness only hinted at when we first began. For in the end, we are in a world of absolute bliss: of material satisfaction, even abundance, but most especially in a world of love beyond the ravages of time. The opening verse talked of lacking nothing, and by the end we have come full circle, but the meaning of God's care has been incredibly expanded in the journey.

Our acquiescence to the message of the poem, our willingness to believe its reality, is accomplished by the poet in the movement through the two metaphors that compose the psalm, a movement that flows from the

---

4. Dahood, *Psalms 1–50*.

most everyday concerns to visions of ultimate redemption. The poet begins with the concrete, the "animal" concerns of the human, and moves to eternity, the most spiritual of claims. The wishes and dreams that underlie the poem have been expressed with such a sense of naturalness that we can almost touch them. As so often in psalms, hope has been made real, words have brought future possibility into reality—the worlds of wish and dream have been made present so that they can be experienced, here and now.

One of the ways the poet accomplishes this artful connection of future and present, abstraction and concretization, is through the seamless flow that takes place in the poem. Despite the division into two distinct metaphors, two stanzas, the movement from one image to the other is maintained through a continuity of thought. As we remarked earlier, the last line of the first image talks about the danger facing the sheep and the protection offered by the shepherd. The second part of the poem begins with a table being set in the face of enemies. For a moment, we might even imagine that the good shepherd has set a formal table for his sheep. We aren't told where we are. It takes a forward-looking moment, a quick glance to the end of the poem, for us to realize that the image has changed, and that now a human guest is in God's house, and that sheep would not be sitting at a table. The seamless flow of ideas is part of the skill of the poet and allows the metaphors to play off each other in a way that gives the poem its unity and makes the dreamlike ending feel as real as the concrete images of the beginning.

It is not an accident that across the centuries this poem has become the locus of our most fervent wishes—able to offer us reassurance at some of our most difficult moments. It is a poem about the extension of the lines of care and love into an infinite and eternal horizon. Out of the concreteness of our physical reality there is a leap to a vision of fulfillment—a leap which we are poetically eased into making ourselves. We live in a world filled with blessing, and as we extend the almost infinite lines of reality into the future what we can imagine as the most wonderful blessing is living intimately with God in the fullness of time.

The power of the psalmist is his ability to create worlds out of words—to make fantasy real, to make the dream of redemption something we can touch and feel.

PART 2

Despair

7

Psalm 27

Disintegration

THE PSALMS WE EXAMINED in Part 1 are replete with the sense of God's presence, God's goodness and care, and the hope in God's justice, but strikingly, the book of Psalms also includes descriptions of other, darker human moments: expressions of abandonment, the confrontation with realities that question faith, the experience of despair that there is no personal salvation. As much as there are psalmists who can feel the presence of God in their every step, in all their wakeful hours, even in their sleep and dreams, psalmists who can express that sense of presence in celebratory, joyous poetry, there are others who look out on the world and see only the bleakness of their own fate: when they think of God, it feels like they face an abyss; their relationship to God is ruptured.

The crisis of faith I am describing resides in three moments. First, there is the sense that the world does not reflect its Creator. God is in the heavens, and God's presence on earth is hardly encountered. In its most abstract formulations, the Bible insists that God is unseen, incomparable to any visible beings, above creation. That abstraction can lead to an overwhelming sense of distance—it is easy to feel that such a God is aloof, perhaps unconscious of or uncaring about our individual human fates. God has become so invisible, so different from anything we humans can recognize, that relationship is hardly possible. And this leads to the second motif in the loss of faith—my life feels meaningless because I have no sense that God has touched it. Sometimes, a psalmist will say that illness and pain has been his fate and the lack of health and well-being has robbed him of any ability to see life as a gift; sometimes a psalmist will experience the world outside as an enemy, out to entrap her, and therefore will despair of experiencing the world as a blessing, containing good; other psalmists offer a more psychological explanation and reveal an inner sense of abandonment, of loneliness, of emptiness. But the absence of God is not only described in personal terms. There is a third motif, less explicitly personal, intertwined with these complaints: God's justice, the promise of moral order implicit and explicit in biblical faith, is nowhere visible in the world.

Thus, the experience of the reality of our lives frequently challenges the claims of faith. Oftentimes, the nonbeliever can rightfully laugh at the faith of the pious because all the evidence of contemporary society is that the religious claim of God's presence, God's care, God's involvement in human affairs is daily disproved by the circumstances of life.

The wonder of psalms is that so many psalmists are willing to face these questions head-on, are willing to express their despair openly and declare that God is absent, that the world is unjust, that corruption reigns and that I am lost.

Almost all the psalms that verbalize these ideas arrive at some resolution at the end: they rediscover the significance of faithfulness.[1] What is quite remarkable, though, is that frequently they do so having arrived at a new understanding, a new formulation as to the meaning of faith. Some of these new formulations are unique in the Bible, some reflect theologies found elsewhere and many of these theological formulations depart from what may be considered the biblical norm. Whether objectively unique or not, certainly, many psalmists talk of arriving at a new insight, a transformed understanding of the meaning of God's caring presence.

In the chapters that follow, I want to explore some psalms that delineate the crisis most strongly, and also look at some of the new, sometimes radical, theologies psalmists evince.

I begin this survey with a discussion of Psalm 27 because the poem itself is a bridge, forming an arc between confidence and despair. The poet begins by expressing her faithfulness, but gradually we are witness to a poet coming apart, a person of faith increasingly in touch with her desperation as she expresses her awareness of God's absence. Back and forth she goes between expressions of her faithfulness and increasingly desperate declarations of her sense of God's desertion—so much so, that by the end, we feel

---

1. Famously, Psalm 88 is a catalogue of despair with no response. For that reason, the psalm feels to many readers like a poem missing an ending.

as if we have received a soldier's final SOS from the foxhole. The war image is not incidental, the poet herself uses it throughout the psalm, but interestingly, by the end we sense an author at war with herself. Increasingly, the author of Psalm 27 is willing to give expression to the felt silence of God, while clinging with her fingers to a message of hope.

PSALM 27

1   A Davidic Psalm.
Adonai is my light and my salvation;
whom shall I fear?
Adonai is the stronghold of my life,
whom shall I dread?

2   When evil people assail me
to devour my flesh
it is they, my besiegers and enemies,
who stumble and fall.

3   If an army mount against me,
my heart would not fear;
should war beset me,
in this, I would have confidence.

4   A single request would I make of Adonai,
that would I seek:
that I might live in the house of Adonai
all the days of my life,
to calmly gaze upon Adonai,
to visit His great hall.

5   For were He to conceal me in His hut on an evil day,
hide me in the enclosure of His tent,
I would be raised as on a high fortress.

6   Now, should He raise my head
above my enemies roundabout,
I would sacrifice in His tent to trumpet blasts,
singing and chanting a hymn to Adonai.

7   Hear my voice as I cry out, Adonai,
favor me, answer me.

8   Of you, my heart says: "Seek my face!"
Adonai, I seek Your face.

9   Do not hide Your face from me;
     do not push aside Your servant in anger.
     You have been my help,
     do not forsake me,
     do not abandon me,
     God of my salvation.

10   Though my father and my mother abandon me,
     Adonai would gather me in.

11   Show me Your way, Adonai,
     and lead me on a straight path
     despite those ranged against me.

12   Do not subject me to the people who besiege me,
     for false witnesses and vicious accusers have appeared against me.

13   Had I not trusted that I might see the goodness of Adonai in the
     land of the living . . .

14   Hope in Adonai;
     strengthen yourself, be of courageous heart,
     hope in Adonai.

In Psalm 27 the battle between hope and faith on the one hand, and the disconsolate condition of the poet on the other, energizes the movement of the poem. As we hear the poet's assertion of faith and then her description of her own actual fate, it gradually dawns on us that her proclamation of faithfulness at the beginning of the poem masks her desperation. Slowly, as the poem unfolds we discover how self-confident assurance hides the urgent fears of the devotee. God's help is asserted in the opening of the poem as having occurred, as being fully assured, yet in the end we understand that this is simply the self-proclamation of the poet, and that in fact her condition is one of needing help, rather than of assurance deriving from help already proffered. What begins as self-confident faith moves in the course of the poem to a hope that has almost no reason to be; the poem proceeds from faithful proclamations to desperate cries to God. Poetic rhetoric, the ability to speak any words that would make sense, almost ends in verse 13, where the completion of the line simply hangs in the air. And then, interestingly, the psalm concludes with a voice that twice utters the word "hope."

Let us start at the beginning. The first three lines of the poem form a single unit of absolute faithfulness. The psalmist is sure that God's presence will always protect her—that she cannot be defeated. The future is absolutely bright because nothing can arise that would endanger her. The past is a record of uninterrupted grace from God. There can be few more self-assured lines in the book of Psalms.

Yet there is a hint of the internal war that we are soon to witness in the choice of rhetorical questioning as the means of expressing this faith. Were the lines to be written to map out their meaning they might be placed on opposite sides of the page, to form an antiphonal response.

> Adonai is my light and my salvation;
> > whom shall I fear?
> Adonai is the stronghold of my life,
> > whom shall I dread?

The faith expressed here is absolute. It can be asked as a rhetorical question because the response is assumed: God will be there for the righteous, at the right side of the faithful. The poet will further articulate her self-confidence in the next two verses. But posing this faith statement as a question, even as a purely rhetorical one, begins the act of opening up the fissure between the assertion of faith and the reality of the poet's life. Questions, after all, admit of differing responses. And later the poet will confess that she is subject to fear and dread, that in fact she feels besieged but unsure of the outcome and suffers from the terrifying sense that God is missing. From the standpoint of what we are about to learn, these opening lines standing in opposition to each other, can be read as harbingers of the internal war about to be enunciated.

The absolute and naive faith of the opening lines begins to be undercut as a new poetics introduces a wish, the first hint of a lack in the life of the poet.

> A single request would I make of Adonai,
> that would I seek:
> that I might live in the house of Adonai
> all the days of my life,
> to calmly gaze upon Adonai,
> to visit His great hall.

There is an innocence in this appeal: I miss only one thing—to see you. It is an expression of a wonderful yearning, of a lover for a beloved, a child for a parent: "I just want to be with you, to hang around you, to walk with you through your house, to see how you live. That moment would offer me some tranquility. What I want is peace and grace." It is a request stated in a soft voice: "God, I want only one thing." And that request can hardly be understood as selfish; rather it is a plea for relationship. Once again, later, we will discover that these softly spoken words conceal deeper meanings, the prayer for tranquility hides the degree to which the author is embattled—the degree to which peace is absent.

> For were He to conceal me in His hut on an evil day,
> hide me in the enclosure of His tent,
> I would be raised as on a high fortress.

The thought of being protected by God, of being alone with God, is enough to restore the poet's joy even though the note of danger has been sounded. Observe here that the self-confident voice has been moved off center: no longer is it simply assured that God will intervene—now there is a plea for God's help. We learn for the first time that the condition of the poet is not as she self-assuredly described it in the first stanza, that of constantly being fed by God's grace, but instead, God's presence is something she desires, something she lacks, without which she feels exposed. The fortress is not guaranteed, rather its appearance is hoped for.

Note too that an interesting movement has taken place: a spiritualization has occurred. Whereas in the opening verses there was a sense of danger from without (metaphors of battle and war were utilized to remark on the defeat of enemies), now the poet speaks of moving inside. It will be sufficient to be closeted with God. Victory will be to stand in God's house, then I would be taller than any enemy, and thus would they be defeated. The poet expresses the wish to be concealed, enclosed, enwrapped; then, with this reassurance, she would be able to emerge into the world, raised high upon a fortress. The poet seeks a moment of inwardness before entering the world; that meeting with God would afford the necessary strength to feel triumphant.

The images used to describe God's sanctuary are fragile ones—God's hut, God's tent. Tents and huts are transient constructions, the latter is portable, the former seasonal. These are hardly the words one would expect to describe a fortress. God's care, though, is the sturdiest thing on which one can depend. In this paradox lies the essential understanding of the faithful: the holy is diaphanous, thin, fragile, yet the spiritual is more significant than all the heaviness and solidity of the material world. In the realm of the religious, that which cannot be seen grants the deepest strength, that which is hidden provides the greatest defense.

In biblical history God's residence changes from a tent to a hut to a kingly throne room. The Bible relates all of these as dwelling places of God: first, the tent of meeting where God spoke to Moses, then, the temporary house at Shiloh where the ark rested before David moved to Jerusalem, and, finally, the imperial temple of Solomon. The psalmist equalizes all these, as if to say: though the place may be temporary, portable, and subject to the elements, nevertheless because God dwells within it, it has the same sturdiness as the stone temple. The human, made up of outer skin, open face, beating heart, is similar. We may be fragile, but our strength depends on our mind, our soul, our spiritual heart. The person of faith may have greater strength than the armor provided soldiers. It is not the outer form but the inner life that creates the most significant protection. God's place can be equally imposing whether it is an elaborate building or a flimsy construction. What is critical is what is hidden, not the skin, the covering, which is revealed. To find God's throne room within is to find peace—the facade is meaningless.

Note too that the images are in descending order, from most to least permanent: earlier the poet spoke of visiting God's "house," now of a "hut," and then, finally, of a "tent." It is as if we are moving back in history to find the primal moment of Israel's relationship with God.

These musings on inwardness and religious vision are interrupted by very practical considerations of what awaits the poet: a reality filled with danger, enemies roundabout.

> Now, should He raise my head
> above my enemies roundabout,
> I would sacrifice in His tent to trumpet blasts,
> singing and chanting a hymn to Adonai.

If the sublime would occur, if I could feel God's protection, be in God's tent, then all that is dangerous, all that is threatening, would not matter. Interestingly, the poet insists on using the word "Now," even though this prayer for the future ought to more precisely be expressed as "Then." This wish is made fully present as if it were a contemporary reality. In the presentness, in the now of wishing and dreaming the truest realities may be found.

If wishes could come true, if that which is secret and hidden could be revealed, if God's presence could be experienced, then joy would burst forth. Singing and dancing would be the order of the day.

But the hidden is not revealed; God is not a felt presence but a perceived absence. Reality contradicts the inner life of the faithful. The religious life is conducted in light of paradox; inner wish, faithfulness, and outer reality are not congruent. And so the poet turns from musing, from wishing and dreaming, to prayer, addressing God directly in the second person and making explicit what it would mean to dwell in God's house:

> Of You, my heart says: "Seek My face!"
> Adonai, I seek Your face.
>
> Do not hide Your face from me;
> do not push aside Your servant in anger.
> You have been my help,
> do not forsake me,
> do not abandon me,
> God of my salvation.

We have traveled a long way from the opening lines of the poem where God is referred to as "my light and my salvation." Now the poet is ready to admit that God is not present for her. Instead of the devotee's being hidden in God's house, it is God who is hidden. The current circumstance of the poet is the experience of God's absence. The psalmist in fact will now plead, "Do not abandon me, God." The author has finally let go of her inhibitions and addresses God directly, expressing her sense of abandonment and turning away from the repeated pieties of received faith. She begins to confront the anguish hidden in her heart.

The insistence on the possibility of God's presence despite the internal experience of absence is emphasized in this stanza with reference to the face of God repeated three times within three lines. The face of a person is the entryway into their subjective life. It is through a smile, through subtle changes of expression, and above all, through the eyes that we discern a person's thoughts and feelings, which words sometimes only hint at, or mask. The entreaty to see God's face is a plea to enter this inward place—to find understanding, to come to know God fully and thereby find comfort. I do not only want the life of faith, of living only with my own thoughts of you; I want to know you, to relate to you, to feel that you are with me.

The repetitions emphasize how single-minded the poet's concentration on God is, and this almost obsessive feeling now achieves its unique expression in the most radical statement of trust we can imagine:

> Though my father and my mother abandon me,
> Adonai would gather me in.

The faith of the psalmist in God is stronger than her belief in any human relationship, even the most fundamental. All earthly relationships are transient; the relationship with God is that which is never failing, eternal. Even the most secure of human relationships, that of parent and child, is still subject to human frailty, whereas the one with God can always be depended on. God will "gather me in" with stronger arms than any parent has. (I understand the expression to be physical rather than otherworldly, though the Hebrew has the same ambiguity as the English, equally evoking death.)

Except for this faith, the poet is, in fact, lost, not knowing how to navigate the realities of life with its mixtures of good and evil.

> Show me Your way, Adonai,
> and lead me on a straight path
> despite those ranged against me,
>
> Do not subject me to the people who besiege me,
> for false witnesses and vicious accusers have appeared against me.

"Show me Your way," is the plea of the person who sees human reality as a puzzle. The right way is hidden, camouflaged; power is corrupt. There is no human appeal for justice that can be made to the courts when the witnesses have been bribed. How can my voice have resonance in the public square, when the messages of faithlessness dominate the public media?

The face of God is hidden, and since this is the case, any real, let alone ultimate, understanding of the world is foreclosed, even to the faithful. Yet, is that not our desire: to know our place (to understand our relationship to the universe, to comprehend the meaning of our lives), the consequence of our deeds? Why is the fulfillment of this wish forever foreclosed to us? What meaning does life have if we can never comprehend the right way, if we can never see the ultimate reality: God?

What the pious experience, then, is that belief in God is a life of faithfulness, it is a service to the Unseen One that seemingly has no visible correlation in this world. Faithfulness has to be sufficient for sustenance. The verbal repetitions throughout the poem emphasize this increasing internalization of faithfulness. The word "heart" is repeated twice, "hidden-ness," three times. The poet knows God in the hidden recesses of her heart.

But can one live that way, without any outer correlation for one's belief?

The final cry of the poet, "Would that I could see God in the land of the living . . ." is a cry of the heart that cuts through all the self-confident assertion of the poem: I trust in God, but that faith is so hard for me, because there is no manifestation of God in any visible reality in this world. Do I have to wait for death in order to be vindicated? Is that not too late? Of what use would such vindication be if I cannot be assured of God's presence, here, in this world?

> Had I not trusted that I might see the goodness of Adonai in the land of the living . . .

The New Jewish Publication Society Translation simply inserts three dots after the word "living," emphasizing that this verse is an internal musing of the author that breaks off before completion. The Hebrew poetic line is missing its parallel counterpoint. It is as if the author has censored herself, as if she would not allow the thought to achieve completion—I might have joined the ungodly—that life is so fetching; for after all, God's deniers are seemingly vindicated by all that occurs in the world around us—but . . .

Faith is contrary to the evidence of reality, it is asserted even amid the feeling of absence and abandonment. Nevertheless, it is faith that has the power to sustain the poet. God's time is not human time, and therefore the devotee remains with the terrible question of whether God will respond within the frame of a human lifetime. In Hebrew, this line, this cry from the heart, is emphasized by the very sounds of the words since the syllables of the first words are liquid and those of the last two, guttural. Thus the syllables of the first half are formed through the lips and the frontal part of the tongue, while the latter can only be sounded by pulling at the back of the throat while opening the mouth wide. So, the sentence moves us to issue a cry from the deep: it is the very bowels of the poet that bellow, "in the land of the living." The sense of opposition, of tearing at herself, which has been so much a part of this poem, is thus emphasized in this penultimate line: "God, I know that You are present for us, but your time is not our time. You may not respond in human terms; I have faith in you: You are my fortress, yet you are the Absconding One, the Disappearing One, the Hidden One. I need to see You. I need You, yet You are nowhere to be found. The consciousness of You is present in the deepest recesses of my heart. Allow my faithfulness to have some correlate in reality. Show yourself to me, in some way—in my lifetime." The poet's loyalty is borne amid desperation.

And then we have a response. Not a response by God, but a response by someone close by.

> Hope in Adonai;
> strengthen yourself, be of courageous heart,
> hope in Adonai.

Who says this last line? Is the voice external or internal? Is it the poet speaking to herself? Is it a chorus telling the poet not to despair? Are these words sufficient to satisfy the poet's hunger, or are they the pat slogans of the pious? Who speaks?

In the end, the authoritative voice of the poet has fissured. Some voice addresses her, as if from the outside, even if its source may be some inner place. There is a rent between her trust in God and the reality of her lonely despair, and she has become split between the two. Ultimately, we realize that the simply stated faith expressed at the beginning of the poem has undergone intense trial, and the poet is left almost broken. The voice of hope is sounded alongside the notes of despair. Both are intensely felt by the poet. The question at the opening of the poem is now no longer rhetorical: by the end a fissure has opened in the heart of the poet.

The poem begins with the personal name of God: *yod*, *heh*, *vav*, *heh*; and the very last word of the poem is the personal name of God. The poet has voiced to us how God-centered her inner life is, but the distance traveled between the opening and closing lines is enormous. The self-confident assertions of the beginning of the poem are replaced by doubt and confusion. Instead of being the assured proclaimer of faith, the poet herself needs to be exhorted to remain faithful. Rather than the brazen, "whom would I fear," with its absolute faith, there is now the need to buck up courage, to hope.

The poet of Psalm 27 has moved from pride to humility. Faith has been replaced by hope. Faith believes absolutely in its rightness. Hope understands that though the evidence is to the contrary, though there is much room for doubt, nevertheless, the faithful manage to live with expectation. Faith is brazen, hope is humble.

What we want is now; what we receive is the futurity of promise. What is wanted is manifestation, revelation, vision; what is received is less than that—wish and dream. The poem ends where the human condition begins, in the glance toward the future, in the dreaming. True faith is faithfulness—the patience of waiting, the satisfaction with hidden things, the living with inwardness.

Reaching the end of the poem, we realize that faith and despair have been at war with each other, that each assertion of faithfulness on the part of the poet has been undercut by an underlying question. With each new stanza, the power of the question increases so that by the end of the poem we discern the full extent of the poet's fears. Finally, we cannot tell if the poet herself is able to respond to her own negativity or whether a priest or chorus needs to prompt the psalmist.

A voice assures the meaningfulness of hope. The voice of tradition? A remembered inner voice? One aspect of our selves? Religious authorities? It is a voice that addresses us from within and without.

We too hear this line spoken from within and without. When we read the psalm, we speak the words of this line and so become the reassuring chorus, reassuring ourselves. The work of our own heart, tortured though it may be, becomes the instrument for the objectifying power of speech, voicing words for living with faithfulness. The tradition speaks in our recitation of these words, as we say to ourselves, "Hope . . ." The promise of the future responds to the question of the present.

And then the poem turns in on itself Möbius-like: for if one had such faith, why would one fear?

8

Psalm 42

The Torn Soul

PSALM 27 IS A poem of increasing disintegration: its penultimate thought expresses the felt absence of God even as its ending articulates a faithful expectation and hope. This swing of emotions is imitated in Psalm 42. Like many other psalms, it does not trace a movement in a single direction but rather gives voice to a balancing of emotions; self-doubt and turmoil are expressed alongside faithful declarations, and this turmoil becomes the explicit subject of the psalm. We are party to an inner dialogue in which the poet constantly moves back and forth, enunciating a yearning for God on the one hand, and despair as to his condition on the other. Readers understand that we are confronting the inner life of a torn soul. Like Psalm 27, Psalm 42 expresses a central plea to see God, and that unfulfilled wish becomes almost a sickness of the soul.

The setting of Psalm 42 is personal exile; the temple in Jerusalem, the center of religious life, is memory. Exile is not merely a physical condition but is a spiritual crisis. Indeed, homelessness ought never to be understood as simply a failure to find shelter, rather to be without a home is to be unanchored, at sea, lost. Psalm 90, which we will discuss later, begins, "the Lord is my refuge": when I feel the presence of God, then I am at home in the universe, but without that I am lost in the world, I am adrift. The loss of the experience of God's presence is felt as a terrifying emptiness within ourselves. Similarly, exile from the temple is a loss of the ability to sense God's closeness and therefore an experience of losing one's center.

Joy, Despair, and Hope

PSALM 42

1   *Of the conductor, A maskil to the Korahites.*[1]

2   As a stag yearns for a stream suddenly bursting forth,
    so my soul yearns for You, O God.

3   My soul thirsts for God, the living God,
    when will I come and appear before God?

4   Night and day, my bread was my tears,
    for each day people said to me, "Where is your God?"

5   This I recall as I pour out my soul:
    how I would travel by pavilion,
    wending my way to God's house,
    joining with celebrating crowds singing joyously and thankfully.

6   Why are you bent over, O my soul?[2]
    Why are you moaning within me?
    Wait upon God,
    for I still acknowledge Him.
    Victories precede Him.

7   My God,
    my soul is bent over,
    as I think of You
    in the land of Jordan and Hermon,
    on Mount Mitzar,

8   where deep calls to deep
    amidst the sound of Your cataracts,
    and all Your waves and breakers pour over me.

9   By day, may Adonai command His love for me,
    and in the evening, may He sing lullabies to me—
    that is my prayer to the God of my being,

1. The Korahites were evidently a Levitical family (they may have been a priestly family who emigrated from northern Israel), and a series of psalms are ascribed to them. No one quite knows the meaning of the technical term *maskil*, which occurs many times in psalmic headings.

2. The word *nefesh*, which is here translated "soul," most often means "person" in the Bible—the whole person, the embodied person. Here, though, this word for "person" has been turned entirely inward and is best rendered in English only as "soul" since the English word simultaneously conveys the notion of person as well as internal consciousness which is so much the subject of this poem.

10 that would I say to God, my rock.

   Why have you forgotten me,
   why must I walk in darkness,
   oppressed by my enemies?

11 Slaughtering me to the bone,
   my besiegers ridicule me,
   as each day, they ask, "Where is your God?"

12 Why are you bent over, O my soul?
   Why are you moaning within me?
   Await God
   for I still acknowledge Him.
   Victory will go before me
   and my God.[3]

From the very first we are greeted with an image of intense but unmet desire. An animal searches for water, instinctively knowing that a spring may suddenly appear anywhere, bubbling forth unpredictably. The animal's thirst drives it on, now searching here, now there. Sometimes it simply stands still, listening for the gurgling sound that will reveal the location of the surging water. At other times it steps slowly, its face to the ground, as if trying to sniff out what it seeks. Unsatisfied, the increasing thirst drives the animal wildly forward. One can watch it on the hilltop, now with its antlers bent down to the ground, now racing onward its antlers plunging forward.

  This thirst-driven seeking is a mixture of hope and pain. If I were to translate the animal's search into human terms, I would say something like this, as hopeful remonstrance tempers moments of desperation: I am conscious of my lack, of my need; and, at the same time, all my experience tells me that my satisfaction is to be found if I but look precisely enough. Keep

3. Many scholars assume that Psalm 43 is the continuation of Psalm 42. There is a commonality of language, the outstanding example of which is the repetition of the chorus at the end of both psalms. Added to this, Psalm 43 is the only psalm in this section (psalms 42–72) which does not have a superscription. Yet, these scholars have been unable to explain why the tradition has, in fact, preserved these two poems as separate psalms. I think that Psalm 43 is written as a response to Psalm 42 rather than being its continuation. As my analysis of Psalm 42 will show, the poem feels entirely integrated and has a quite satisfactory ending. The play with the internalization of the divine, which is characteristic of Psalm 42 and which culminates with a wish for God's appearance in that psalm is quite different than the hoped-for end of Psalm 43, which depicts a revived temple worship.

looking; it is there. You can feel those emotions as you watch the animal gracefully cocking its head from side to side at the crest of the hill, now sniffing the ground, now looking from side to side, finally fixing its face forward. In the Judean desert, aquifers carry water from the mountains. It may not have rained in the desert, but suddenly a spring bubbles up, rushing water spills down ravines, as the rain that has fallen in the mountains rushes underground, carried down to the sea. No one can anticipate where and when these rushing waters will appear, but life in the desert depends on them. I am thirst-driven, too, says the poet,

> so my soul yearns for You, O God.

But my sense of deprivation is worse than that of the animal, for my condition is not merely a physical torment, but my lack is spiritual; it is seen as a condemnation of you, God.

> Night and day, my bread was my tears,
> for each day people said to me, "Where is your God?"

For the one in exile, the truths known in the soul cannot be communicated to those at hand. There was an experience of home that cannot be captured in this foreign land—the tastes, the smell, even the quality of light was different. When I describe my religious life to the people here, they know nothing of what it was like to be with God, to experience that joy of feeling in God's presence, being in God's care. And so the poet expounds on the memory of home.

> This I recall as I pour out my soul:
> how I would travel by pavilion,
> wending my way to God's house,
> joining with celebrating crowds singing joyously and thankfully.

Some of the Hebrew is difficult, and disagreements about the exact translation have continued since ancient times. And yet the sense is unmistakable. There was a time when I felt I could reach God; I remember the rejoicing on a holiday in the temple. The entire congregation felt moved by the moment, we all felt we were seeing God. The author contrasts this remembered time when all was right in the world with a current sense of abandonment: I was a man of wealth then, traveling to Jerusalem in luxury, joining the crowds coming to express their thanks; religious life was filled with joyful singing. Now, though, the author sits on the other side of the Jordan, in the mountains of Lebanon beyond the Galilee. Home can only be dreamed of. Here everything feels oppositional. The poet uses an image that turns standard biblical metaphors on their head: he talks of the water flowing in the mountains, of the noise it makes as it breaks over the rocks. It can be seen as an image of plenty, of the glory of God's creation, and indeed the poet says that, "deep calls to deep," thus echoing other biblical references to the way nature celebrates its Creator. Yet his experience of these sounds is that they are dangerous: he is caught in the waterfall and is in fear of drowning.

> My God,
> my soul is bent over,
> as I think of You,
> in the land of Jordan and Hermon,
> on Mount Mitzar,
>
> where deep calls to deep
> amidst the sound of Your cataracts,
> and all your waves and breakers pour over me.

The wished-for water with which the poem began is a threat rather than a blessing. Now, high in the mountains amid the waterfalls, at the source of the region's flowing water, it rushes with such force that there is no succor, only danger. These are not the still, placid, waters to which the tender shepherd of Psalm 23 leads her flock. Rather these are waters that may drown the sheep. Nature, God's creation, is an enemy rather than a friend. We know of no mountain named Mitzar, and the name may simply be a play on the Hebrew, *tza-ar*, meaning "trouble" and "pain." The poet is in the land of pain, in exile, and in exile even that which was meant for salvation, water, becomes an instrument of destruction, something terrifying, something to be feared.[4]

All the poet has now is the memory of a time when the nearness to God was palpable. Even if God is not present at this moment, there was a time when the presence of God was firmly sensed. I know that. I once experienced it; it can come again. On the other hand, that very knowledge is painful: once I felt the joy of the successful pilgrimage; now I experience only my lack. I can never make peace with this exile, for I know what the good life is. I once experienced it. Memory, that function so central to biblical theology, to Israel's existence, is a two-edged sword. When feelings

---

4. I am grateful to Steven Geller, the biblical scholar, for the suggestion regarding the name Mitzar (oral communication).

of loss overwhelm us, recalling even once-joyous moments can be painful rather than consoling.

But the poet does not dwell on this distress. Instead he loses himself in a world of dream:

> By day, may Adonai command His love for me,
> and in the evening, may He sing lullabies to me—
> that is my prayer to the God of my being,
> that would I say to God, my rock.

The wish is for an idealized future. The past is a memory of bringing gifts to God, of the congregation singing, the future is an idealized image of God acting lovingly towards the faithful, of God's singing lullabies at night so that sleep is easy, untroubled. Instead of Levites singing to God, God will take up song and sing to his creation, the pilgrim.

This is the only time in the poem where God is addressed by God's personal name, Adonai. It is also the only moment in the poem where the direct address to God shifts from lament to plea. The poet specifically describes this moment as one of prayer. Because of these critical differences from the rest of the poem, some scholars have argued that this line is a later interpolation, a pious gloss by an interpreter. I prefer to see it as intrinsic, an integral part of the twisting and turning of mood that takes place in almost every line of the poem. Prayer and complaint, hope and dread, joy and pain, live side by side in this poem.[5]

In fact, this momentary, touching image of security, peace, and calm, of God singing to the child at night, is followed by the most violent images: light is gone; murder threatens.

> Why have you forgotten me,
> why must I walk in darkness,
> oppressed by my enemies?
>
> Slaughtering me to the bone,
> my besiegers ridicule me,
> as each day, they ask, "Where is your God?"

The most piercing attack the enemies perpetrate against the poet is the question, "Where is your God?" I trust in You, I have faith in You, You are a

---

5. The same scholars who would combine Psalms 42 and 43 would see this verse as an interpolation. The same motive is behind both. They fail to see that what is wished for here is expressed as a longing for the presence of God.

stronghold, the very center of my life, yet You are nowhere to be found. The distress caused by Your absence breaks my bones, makes me feel as if I walk through a world without light, as if my throat is squeezed to choking. God is absent and so the poet declaims: I have no correlate for my faith.

Exile means that I am condemned to hold onto a remembered truth that I find impossible to demonstrate.

The expressed yearning for God has both an inner correlate and an objective manifestation. There is an inner sense of life being bereft, no longer touched by God. The internal abandonment is matched by an outer abandonment: the author also insists that his enemies say, "Where is your God?" Presumably, in addition to the poet's longing for a personal revelation, there needs to be some outer manifestation as well: God's appearance would mean that they would see that my life is not empty, that I prosper, that society reflects a divine order in some way—most especially that justice is served, that religious institutions reflect the holiness to which they are committed, so that we all, once again, proceed to the temple joyfully, as one congregation. These latter possibilities are hardly even hinted at in this poem. I presume them on the basis of other biblical and especially psalmic references: here only vague allusions are offered. What is central is the internal yearning, the hope for God's presence.

Now the poet repeats the refrain that has become the chorus of the psalm with its central line: "Await God, for I still acknowledge Him." God's presence is not only a memory, a reality that is past, but there is a life with God in the very act of faithfulness.

Exile will not be forever. And here the poet appeals to the same frame of mind that ended Psalm 27: hope. The Hebrew word used here, *ho-hi-li* meaning "wait" is synonymous with the word used in Psalm 27, *ka-veh*, meaning "hope." *Ho-hi-li* is similarly used in Genesis to describe Noah's waiting for the land to dry up. One waits with very precise expectation. Every good thing needs time to unfold. The stag searches for water; what wonderful pleasure when he finds it! At such a moment, perhaps he can hear singing in his ear. Wait and know that a time of deliverance is coming. Your hope is not based on nothing. After all, there once was a time when joy was palpable. Will it not come again?

The line arguing that one remain hopeful, faithful, occurs twice in the poem, but in the last line the phrasing is slightly different from what had appeared earlier. In verse 6, the poet says "Victories precede Him"; that is, God's entry into the world will mean that evildoers will finally be overturned. But now, in verse 12, the author says, "Victory will go before me and my God." God's appearance will justify me and all I have waited for. Your presence, God, would not only be Your victory, it would be mine.

But this line can also be read independently and thus can imply an even further assertion: my faithfulness already constitutes my victory. My own face reflects the knowledge that hope in God is my salvation, and so its outer visage now is one of victory. I have been faithful, and so I have already won over my enemies. My faithfulness is my victory, God, and Yours.

9

Psalm 77

Memory

IN THE BACKGROUND OF Psalm 42 is the allusion to the memory of another time. Now the poet sits in exile, but there is a remembrance of the joy-filled pilgrimage to Jerusalem. In Psalm 77 there is a different kind of remembering balancing despair: the memory of the events that formed the people Israel—national memory rather than personal memory.

The Jewish theologians Martin Buber and Franz Rosenzweig described an important rhetorical device underlying biblical poetics. As they began to translate the Bible from Hebrew into German, a work of remarkable achievement, they noticed that a biblical chapter would frequently use the same root word several times. These repetitions seemed to be a ubiquitous literary device—it was as true of prose narratives as poetic passages. So they were careful to translate similar Hebrew words with the same German root each time, in order to alert readers to the repetition, for they came to feel that these words, which they called *key words*, could unlock the meaning of a biblical chapter. In word repetitions, they seemed to discover motifs that the biblical author wanted us to pay attention to. They imagined that biblical culture was primarily oral, and so repetitions formed a critical aspect of biblical poetics since it is a central element of oral rhetorical art. (Whether this last point is true or not for the Bible as a whole, certainly we can imagine most psalms as being a primarily oral art.)

Their insight is important. Noticing key words can help us locate the meaning of psalms whose message would otherwise elude us. Psalm 77 is a good example of a somewhat difficult poem where noticing repetitions unlocks meaning, and the psalm that is recovered through a close reading is surely worth the effort because it will present us with a unique theological moment. Martin Buber himself analyzed this particular psalm and pointed out that the root of the verb *remember* repeats itself three times. The fulcrum of the poem is memory: what we choose to remember and the way memory can help us overcome the pain of the present. Psalm 77 presents us with two different kinds of memory—national and personal—and it will be as if we are asked to choose between them.

But other repeated images and words also tie the psalm together. This is a poem filled with sounds: with the wailing and crying of the author, with the sounds of troops marching and seas tossing. Memory involves the ability to hear an inner voice, and the poet is particularly concerned with what voices we listen to, what it is we hear, for in certain strands of biblical thought, to see God is to listen carefully.

In this psalm the multitude of voices engage an inner argument. What should I remember? What should I think? How do I make sense of my world given the different memories whose voices I hear? What is the relation of my own experience to the experience recorded in received religious traditions? What sense do I make of my suffering? What relationship to God does my suffering allow me to think possible?

In Psalm 77, we are party to an internal dialogue and to the discoveries this self-reflection uncovers.

PSALM 77

1   *For the leader; on Jeduthan, from the Asaph collection, a psalm.*[1]

2   I raise my voice to God, I shriek;
        I raise my voice to God; let Him hear me.

3   In my time of trouble, I searched for my Lord;
        my arm flailed the night, tirelessly;
        I would not be comforted.

4   Remembering God, I moan;
        when I express myself, my spirit collapses. *Selah.*

5   You pulled my eyelids open.
        I was startled, I could not speak.

---

1. No one knows the meaning of the word *Jeduthan*, which may in fact be a proper name. The Asaph psalms form a second major collection along with the Korah psalms we mentioned earlier. The Hebrew *mizmor* is translated in the new JPS version as "psalm" and has the overtone of "song," or "words put to music." We have no idea as to whether it may be a technical term describing a particular poetic form or musical setting.

6 I took account of the past,
   the long ago.

7 Remembering my nightly wail,
   I would talk to myself,
   and examine my own spirit.

8 "Will my Lord hide forever,
   and never again be mollified?

9 Has His love disappeared forever?
   Has He ended relating to each generation?

10 Has God forgotten how to pity?
   Has His anger stifled his compassion?" *Selah*.

11 And I said, "It is my sickness.
   Can Heaven's right arm change?"

12 I remind myself of God's deeds;
   yes, I remind myself of Your wonders of old;

13 I recount all Your works;
   I speak of Your acts.

14 O God, Your ways are holiness;
   what god is as great as God?

15 You are the God who works wonders;
   You have manifested Your strength among the peoples.

16 By Your arm You redeemed Your people
   the children of Jacob and Joseph. *Selah*.

17 The waters saw You, O God,
   the waters saw You and were convulsed:
   the very deep quaked as well.

18 Clouds streamed water;
   the heavens rumbled;
   Your arrows flew about;

19 Your thunder sounded in the spheres;
   lightning lit up the world;
   the earth quaked and trembled.

20 Your way was through the sea,
   Your path, through the mighty waters;
   but where You stepped was never revealed.

21 You led Your people like a flock
   in the care of Moses and Aaron.[2]

2. This is not an easy psalm: some of the Hebrew is difficult, and both medieval and modern commentators and scholars have disagreed on the proper translation. While

We can almost hear the devotee as the opening lines of the psalm are sounded: it is a shriek, a plaintive cry of the soul, a supplication of a broken heart. The psalmist's trouble seems to have extended over a long period of time and resulted in his or her despair over God's ever responding. The pain is so great, it has gone on for so long, that there is only one conclusion the poet can come to: God has disappeared from the world. This is, then, not simply a prayer for help but an accusation against God for God's absence.

Physical pain can lead to a sense of intense loneliness, a feeling that no one understands my condition, that I am abandoned. In extreme pain, a patient may move back and forth between anger and depression.

> In my time of trouble, I searched for my Lord;
> my arm flailed the night, tirelessly;
> I would not be comforted.

The ailment which begins as physical becomes a spiritual crisis.

> Remembering God, I moan;
> when I express myself, my spirit collapses

The anguish of the poet is palpable. It is filled not only with a personal expression of despair but equally with theological despondency. If God has absconded, the very act of prayer is an affliction, a reminder of the uncaring God. "Remembering God, I moan": speech, rather than functioning as communication and therefore offering relief, turns on itself and makes the speaker recognize the futility of any attempt to relate to God. Self-reflection and prayer, rather than offering surcease from pain, has led to spiritual depression.

---

some of the problems make little difference, the obscurity of verse 11, a critical turning point of the psalm, makes the poem especially hard to decipher. Moreover, some modern scholars have felt that the ending is abrupt and that we are missing a continuation of the psalm. While my own feeling is that the psalm works as a poem as we have it, the fact that some feel there are missing elements points to the difficulty that even scholars have had in reading this poem. Reading the psalm in translation, one may not have a sense of these difficulties—since every translation has to make a single choice as to meaning—and it is an interesting exercise to compare translations; one comes upon almost distinct poems. The translation here is based on the new Jewish Publication Society version, though I have revised it in those places where their translation is based on emendations; rather, I have preserved the traditional Hebrew Masoretic readings. I have also tried to insure that the English reader is conscious of the repetitions in the Hebrew—the same English word is always used for the repeated Hebrew root—and I have relied more heavily than elsewhere on traditional Jewish interpretations of the meaning of the individual words and phrases in the psalm.

Then something occurs that transforms the poet: God's presence is acknowledged in the dream of the night.

> You pulled my eyelids open.
> I was startled, I could not speak.

The unusual image the poet uses is strong enough to convey his own sense of being suddenly startled. Something has happened to wake him from his despair, to change the direction of his thought, to move him from his own endless wallowing in gloom. For the first time, he cannot speak. The constant utterance of complaint is halted. It is as if God has told him, "Can't you see!" Literally, God opens his eyes. This startling moment wakes him from his own reverie, from being only absorbed by his own condition. He is now engaged by a new set of thoughts—the contemplation of the God of history, the God of his people, the God of the tradition.

> I took account of the past,
> the long ago.

It is the corporate memory of God's presence that is set against his own experience of God's abandonment. He reviews his own spiritual history, his current bout with despair, and then compares it to what once occurred. He places his narrative alongside the narrative of liberation of the Jewish people. The exodus from slavery is the paradigmatic story of God's response to those in the pit, those at the bottom of the ladder; it is the primal story of the establishment of his people, and its message is that God stands with the downtrodden, the weak, the suffering.

But this psalm will not ultimately reflect a simple theology. The devotee is not silenced. The poet has suffered too deeply for faith to be asserted easily. This is not a poem where the poet acknowledges God and says, "Oh, yes, I forgot my place." Instead, what he now confronts is something less than the immediacy of salvation and more than the total despair he has found himself in: there is a glimmer that allows for the possibility of hope.

What was at first a complaint has now turned into a question: have you stopped helping us? The terrible possibility is that the answer might be yes. But equally there is also a place left in the devotee that allows the possibility of a no: the God who helped us in the past is always present and has not deserted us. If that is true, we ought not despair but instead learn patience, and wait for deliverance, taking comfort in memory.

> Remembering my nightly wail,
> I would talk to myself,
> and examine my own spirit.

> "Will my Lord hide forever,
> and never again be mollified?

In fact, as the poet begins to ruminate on theological possibility, the poet's own complaint has itself become a memory. In verse 7 the psalmist says, "I remembered my nightly wail," As he is startled out of his reverie, there is a distancing from his protest, at the very least it has been turned from a declarative accusation against God to an interrogative.

> Has His love disappeared forever?
> Has He ended relating to each generation?
> Has God forgotten how to pity?
> Has His anger stifled His compassion?

The memory of the deliverance from Egypt cannot wipe away the memory of the poet's own suffering. The faithful rehearse God's past behavior, God's rescue in times gone by. Yet where is God now? Why does salvation not come to the righteous in our time? The two different memories, one evoked by history, the other of his own suffering, create an inner conflict that issues in questions. The opening of the poet's eyes makes him see in new ways but does not offer a simple solution to the problem of suffering and to the question of injustice. A new voice has entered his consciousness, but it has not wiped away the pain of his own condition. The evocation of historical memory, though, is a turning point in the reverie of the poet, allowing for different thoughts—not only the self-evocation of his own pain—to enter the poet's consciousness.

At first it is the memory of the report of God's helping hand that adds to the suffering of the poet. If God once helped, why is God absent now? The contemporary silence of God is overwhelming. Yet it is memory, the rehearsal of the story of God's presence in Israel's history, that will provide the necessary solace for the poet to glimpse hope. The language of the tradition will provide an opening to words of comfort.

> And I said, "It is my sickness.
> Can Heaven's right arm change?"

> I remind myself of God's deeds;
> yes, I remind myself of Your wonders of old;

I recount all of Your works;
I speak of Your acts.

And then in verses 15 to 21 the poet recites the historical story in full detail, borrowing the language of the joyous Song at the Sea. Does not the history of God's response to the suffering of his people hint at the constant saving hand of God? Does not the recitation of the story of the past tell us about our own condition and afford us comfort?

The waters saw You, O God,
the waters saw You and were convulsed:
the very deep quaked as well.

Clouds streamed water;
the heavens rumbled;
Your arrows flew about;

Your thunder sounded in the spheres;
lightning lit up the world;
the earth quaked and trembled.

The memory of the details of the exodus story constitutes the alternative narrative to the psalmist's suffering. And as he tells that story, as the crossing at the sea gains more and more power through the specificity of poetic language, the poet formulates God's presence in a way that holds the answer to his own condition. In the penultimate verse of the poem he says:

Your way was through the sea,
Your path, through the mighty waters;
but where You stepped was never revealed.

This is a fascinating formulation, for in all other tellings of the exodus story the point is that all Israel saw God's mighty arm. If there was ever a moment when Israel came face-to-face with God, it is in the miracle at the sea. When all was thought to be lost, when Pharaoh's chariots had caught up with the escaping Israelites, then the waters tumbled in on the Egyptians. In Exodus these events are described in the most miraculous terms, and echoes of the cataclysm are evoked by the psalmist. The poet, though, points out that even then, at the moment when God was said to have been most clearly involved in transforming history, God was not visible. God's footsteps were invisible.

Tradition has it that the people saw the hand of God—in the words of the later rabbinic sages, even the handmaiden at the Sea saw more than Moses did on Mount Sinai—but the poet declares that to see God is always a matter of belief: even at the highest moment of revelation God was hidden. God is the Diaphanous One, seen only through the lattices of reality. We were saved, but even in our greatest moment of deliverance we never saw God directly; all we saw was Moses and Aaron at the head of the line of march. Even there, God was still the Hidden One. God's seeming hiding now is no different than what seemed manifest long ago. God has always been the Unseen One. This is a unique message of this poet. We will never see God. Even at the Sea, Your footsteps could not be traced.

And so the poem ends:

> You led Your people like a flock
> in the care of Moses and Aaron.

What the people saw was Moses and Aaron leading them. They were cared for and nurtured in the desert; they entered the land and conquered it. Through all this they saw the hand of God, but in reality God's tracks could not be found. God walks the earth, but immediately the trace of God is obliterated by the inundating waves of time. The sea is surrounded by a beach of sand. If you walk the beach, the waves quickly wash away any trace of a presence. There is then nothing to be seen of God after the event. All there ever is of God that can be known by us is an internal sense of presence, and this we may experience even now.

This insight is at the heart of the poet's own spiritual regeneration. It is what woke him up in the middle of the night: God's footsteps are silent, disappearing in the night. The trace of God in the world is an inner voice, a personal turning that allows a human being to open his eyes and see the world differently than before, though these same events might be interpreted otherwise by someone else. God's presence is always unseen, but God opens our eyes to see the world differently—that is what is meant by the presence of God.

Noise and silence alternate with each other in this poem. Words describing speech, voice, internal dialogue, and noise fill this psalm. The root word for "sound" or "voice," *kol*, forms a leitmotif in the poem and is repeated in variant forms five times in the psalm; it is doubled in the same sentence both at the very beginning and toward the end of the psalm. Synonyms for "speech," "sound" and "noise" are constantly used. In fact, it is a test of the translator's art to be able to supply as many varieties of wording in English as the Hebrew does. The psalmist raises up his voice and cries out (verse 2), he remembers his nightly moaning; when he talks of the incident at the sea, he mentions the thunder and the quaking of the land—heaven and earth filled with sound. (The latter images should be especially noted, for what the poet has done to emphasize the image is to conflate the description of the thunder and the quaking of the mountain at Sinai, the moment of revelation, with the crossing of the sea.) The poet *speaks* to himself, *examines* his soul (verse 7) while he *takes account of* the past (verse 6). He *recounts* God's works, and *speaks* about what God has done (verse 13).

As opposed to this cacophony of sound and word are the silences that punctuate the poem and form the paradox that gives rise to the poet's questions. The problem the poet poses is whether God still speaks (verse 9); the poet's plaint is stopped by God's making him see something he had not seen before, and so he "does not speak" (verse 5). It is the moment when the poet stops speaking, when he is startled, that his eyelids are opened, and he is made to see reality in a new way (verse 5).

The language used here for the exodus evokes the most primal forces of nature: thunder, lightning, and churning sea. We are not only at the moment of exodus but in touch with the forces at work in creation itself. Yet this mighty scene leaves no trace of God. We are surrounded by the crashing sounds of these forces but ultimately denied a vision of the God within. And if even at the Sea there was scarcely a trace of God's presence, similarly, there is hardly a trace of God's presence anywhere in creation. The presence of God can only be understood through belief, trust. It is in the silences that we learn to see; it is the perspective with which we view the world, our condition, our past, that allows us to feel God's presence.

God's presence is not subject to demonstration—ever—not even in the most miraculous moments. This is not a poem that asks us to abandon our doubts, only to question our stance and open ourselves to balance these voices with others—voices of history, of the tradition.

It is appropriate that the swing moment of the psalm is filled with interrogative, for the poem is balanced on a question: which voice should I listen to, which memory accurately portrays reality? This is the dilemma of those who adhere to the One whose tracks are immediately erased by the very sea that demonstrates God's presence. The believer never has surety.

And so the poem ends in midair, without resolution. The last words we hear are:

> You led Your people like a flock
> in the care of Moses and Aaron.

The poet does not offer us the image of a cloud and a pillar of fire leading the people as Exodus and Numbers do, but of two human beings the people trusted who were acting on God's behalf. As the prophet Jeremiah says while comforting his people: "I remember the gift of your youth, the love you exhibited in betrothal, when you followed me in the desert, the unseeded land" (Jeremiah 2:2). The faithful origin of the people marching in the desert holds out hope that faith makes sense now, in the desert moment of the soul. Salvation lies in remembering this original moment and holding on to it. In the middle of the night, the poet learns that through a conscious act, he can create words that can be a comfort. He can balance his own pain and suffering by remembering other sounds and sights. The articulation of another time evokes God's presence, even if current experience speaks of the absence of God. Voice is placed over against voice, and a negative experience may be balanced by a positive memory. As he recites the history of his people, the memory of a saving time, the poet achieves a distance from his own sorry state and finds the invisible traces of the hidden God, the Unseen One. In the desert, when Israel accepted the authority of Moses and Aaron as they wandered in the wilderness, they did not feel deserted but cared for.

And we too can recite the words of the poem and find a measure of comfort to soothe our soul, the bearer of our own complaints. And the knowledge that someone else experienced God's absence in similar ways that we may feel now, and then found some comfort in traditional memory, can lead us to feel that reciting the words of the tradition will lead us too to an understanding of the way that God is present in our lives. The poet's ambivalence can match our own and the poet's subtle understanding may revive us as it revived him. Turning to the tradition we too may be startled and suddenly have our eyes opened as we face the question of our lives. As it spoke to this poet, so the silence that torments our soul may speak with pregnant meaning and we may discover that the Absconding God still walks among us, with untraceable steps.

10

Psalm 73

The Psalmic Job

PSALM 77 IS CENTERED on personal complaint—though we are not told its precise source, we imagine pain and illness being the cause of the poet's despair. Other psalms we have examined have focused on the inner experience of the absence of God; these poems have not revealed whether that sense arises out of personal tragedy or lies elsewhere. There is another more public theme out of which biblical authors describe the absence of God: the prevalence of injustice. The existence of God should assure a moral universe. Again and again, the Bible describes God as the one who will judge the corrupt, punish evil, side with the downtrodden, reward the good. Abraham can turn to God and ask, "Shall not the judge of all the earth deal justly?," for the assumption of God's justice is the underpinning of all biblical theology. Israel's story is testimony to that assertion, for the Exodus narrative is told as the story of God hearing the cries of a slave, overturning the oppression of the greatest power of the day, and instructing the people Israel to remember their own suffering and create a just and compassionate society.

The biblical crisis of faith is most critically felt in the experience of the absence of justice. The corruption of the earthly system of justice is a sign of nonbelief, the quintessential act of betrayal of the divine. Equally, an unjust universe is an accusation against God. Should not the God of all the earth repay good and evil? Why does evil seem to prosper, and good seem to issue no reward? Why are the pious the ones who are poor and persecuted? In God's universe, the innocent ought not to suffer, but flourish; evil ought not to rule the public sphere. That the pious suffer beyond what they deserve as punishment for any sin they may have committed is the central dilemma of the book of Job, and it is not only in that book that the question is engaged: it is a central dilemma of biblical faith.

Psalm 73 has an almost Job-like quality as it describes the tension of the life of faith. Here the devotee describes the way in which she herself almost lost her faith. We are offered a window into self-doubt that accompanies the seeker of God when there is no correlation in the outside world to the inner affirmations of the faithful. The first half of the poem is one of the strongest biblical descriptions of the lack of reward for moral behavior, the ethical unfairness of life. The extensive catalogue of complaint contains some of the most poetically powerful, though ironic, passages in Psalms.

Job receives a final revelation that transforms his understanding, and our author too has a vision that is a response to her questioning of God. Scholars and theologians have long debated the ultimate meaning of the book of Job and the implications of its ending. Has God simply overpowered Job? Has the problem of evil been resolved? As in Job, so in the last half of Psalm 73 the proper interpretation is unclear. This much one might say: the psalmic response feels quite different from the response to Job, and it is worth looking at this psalm closely to see how it may offer an alternative to the book of Job.

PSALM 73

1	*A psalm of Asaph.* Surely, good comes to Israel, God to the clear hearted.
2	As for me, my feet almost slipped, I nearly stepped and stumbled,
3	for I envied the dissolute; I saw the wicked at ease.
4	Death has no pangs for them; their body is healthy.
5	They have no part in the travail of humanity; they are not afflicted like other humans.
6	So pride adorns their necks, lawlessness enwraps them as a mantle.

7   Their eyes bulge out of their fat,
     as they survey their hearts' fancies.

8   They scoff and plan evil,
     talking down from their heights.

9   They speak as though from heaven,
     their words going forth on earth.

10   And so the people turn to them,
     drinking up their words.

11   And they say, "How would God know?
     Is there knowledge with the Most High?"

12   Such are the wicked;
     ever tranquil, they amass followers.

13   It was for nothing that I kept a pure heart,
     and washed my hands in innocence,

14   seeing that I have been constantly afflicted,
     that each morning brings new punishments.

15   Had I decided to talk like them,
     I should have betrayed Your disciples.

16   So I applied myself to understand this,
     but it seemed a hopeless task

17   till I entered God's Sanctuary
     and understood their fate.

18   You place them amidst mirages;
     You make them fall through blandishments.

19   How suddenly are they ruined,
     wholly swept away, ended through confusion.

20   Like a dreamer after waking,
     God, when aroused, despises their image.

21   When my heart soured,
     and my feelings were numbed,

22   I was an unknowing fool,
     behaving like an animal toward You.

23   Yet, I was always with You;
     You held my right hand;

24   You guided me by Your counsel
     and will lead me toward honor.

25   Whom else have I in heaven?
     And having You, I want no one else on earth.

26 Though my body and heart fail,
   God is my heart's fortress, my portion forever.

27 Those who keep far from You will be lost;
   You will cut off all who are untrue to You.

28 As for me, nearness to God is good;
   I have made the Lord, Adonai, my refuge,
   to recount all Your works.

The psalm begins with an aphorism, a cliché, a received theological truth:

> Surely, good comes to Israel,
> God to the clear hearted.

The opening sentence exists almost as a moment apart in the psalm, like an epigraph to be read before the beginning of a poem or book. It may be a quotation from another popular psalm or work of wisdom, or it may be the pious creed that has guided the poet till now. There is no verb in the original Hebrew—in Hebrew grammar the missing *is* can be understood without being stated—and so the verse allows itself to be heard as a slogan announcing an absolute identity: Good to Israel, God to the clear hearted. There is no action, only an arrow leading from one noun to the other, a pure identity.

And then the *I* enters, the *I* who overturns all known truths in the crucible of inner testing. "But, I"—"As for me"—with that moment of self-reflection, with that critical "but," the *I* of personal experience is pitted against the slogans of religious tradition. The righteous are supposed to find happiness, fulfillment; well, let me tell you my story, because you're in for a surprise . . . The glory of Psalms is that we can hear this personal voice so clearly, and that we can experience it across the space of more than twenty-five hundred years. This *I* calls to us in its intensity.

The poet is not afraid to admit being swept up in feelings and thoughts that lead her to question, to doubt, the fundamentals of religious faith. This self-reflective person baldly describes being caught up in jealousy. The life of the righteous seems paltry compared to the wonderful lives of the ungodly.

"And I almost . . ." This *almost* is critical. It does double service. On the one hand, it tells us how close to falling from faith we can come, how challenging are the questions, even to the faithful, if one is genuinely prepared to face them. On the other hand, we are forewarned that the story of this tormented soul will not be single-minded. As the questions pile on, we should expect something else to happen, a turning. This will be a poem of faithfulness, but one that does not shrink from facing difficult truths.

The argument the poet puts forward in verses 3–14 builds with ironic power. As in the book of Job, so in Psalm 73 each line of the poet's accusation refutes the standard responses of classic theology. There is no letup from the incessant questioning that torments the poet. The author describes her anguish in overwhelming detail, each line delineating the happiness and well-being of the ungodly, and with each we realize how deprived the poet feels, for the conditions in which the wealthy and powerful live are not at all descriptive of the poet's own life.

The ungodly are really leading the good life. They have wealth, good health; one can't even say that their past catches up with them, for truthfully, many of them don't even die a painful death but expire peacefully at home surrounded by loved ones and the best medical care. In this questioning of theological platitudes, all the favorite rejoinders of the pious are demolished, as, for instance, "The fat cats may look good to you now, but just wait and see how their sins come back to haunt them." Well there is no haunting; the wealthy live happily and die happily, and there is no day of reckoning. Meanwhile, the pious lead troubled lives; they are down and out; they suffer, and they may die in their suffering. Is this the fulfillment of God's promise for the beneficent care of the righteous? There seems to be no ultimate accounting. We can hear the argument against God as the words of the poet pile on, and the distress of the author is palpable throughout this accusatory argument. What is expressed is as sharp and poignant as anything encountered in the book of Job. How can the righteous life be so unrewarded? How can the wicked only prosper?

> Death has no pangs for them;
> their body is healthy.
>
> They have no part in the travail of humanity;
> they are not afflicted like other humans.

The author uses physical imagery to contrast the lives of the sinful and her own wretched existence. Certainly there is a torturous envy of those who appear to be prosperous. Those impious bastards are healthy, so much so that they don't even suffer dying. They put on a little weight and go to wonderful resorts to reduce; they keep in shape, tanning themselves at the spas only the rich can afford. They seem to live on easy street:

> So pride adorns their necks,
> lawlessness enwraps them as a mantle.
>
> Their eyes bulge out of their fat;
> as they survey their hearts' fancies.

What they desire they easily acquire, and their desires seem to have no limit.

> Such are the wicked;
> ever tranquil, they amass followers.

Those in power, those who have wealth, seem to be able to do as they please—they amass riches, care for nothing but themselves, and others, looking at them, want exactly what these haughty people have.

These rich folk poke fun at religious folk; they laugh at traditional morality. It is the poor and the downtrodden who are pious and the rich who make fun of religious involvements.

> They speak as though from heaven,
> their words going forth on earth.
>
> And so the people turn to them,
> drinking up their words.
>
> And they say, "How would God know?
> Is there knowledge with the Most High?"

These powerful people who feed off the poor are the ones who make fun of religion. They pride themselves on their *bon mots* that put down those who have a serious pious inclination. "We are the ones who own the earth, not God." One can hear their irony in the line the poet chooses to put in their mouths: "Is there knowledge with the Most High?" They believe they can get away with anything, and they do. Human acts, and subsequent well being, are the subject of politics and the exercise of power. It is those in power who sustain life not God.

Injustice reigns. God is in the heavens and earthly life reflects not a whit of God's care, only the raw display of wealth and political power. The psalmist confronts a social reality that can bear out none of God's promise. Power is in the hands of an oppressive upper class that will not respond to any moral or religious appeal. The righteous live in poverty, their lives mocked. Justice is absent from the face of the earth. Though the Bible is replete with promises of success in response to obedience to the law, though heaven is supposed to punish wickedness, there is no evidence that this is the rule of life. Instead, reality points the other way: fairness is not an inherent principle in the universe; goodness is hardly rewarded but frequently leads to suffering. To know what the good life looks like, just go and visit with the powerful and wealthy "atheists" (those who do not believe in God's singular power). Reality does not reflect God's promised reward; on the contrary, all the facts point to the opposite. The religious devotee has to confront the terrible knowledge of the absence of God, including the ultimate irony that they—the rich and powerful—don't pay for sin eventually, for they die comfortably, their lives never disturbed by the consequences of their deeds.

And then something happens. This despairing vision that has obsessed the poet is recast. A moment comes that towers over the initial perspective of the poem and effects a total transformation. If we lay the two halves of the poem side by side, then we have two very opposite moods, two very opposite movements. For the poet suddenly enters into a new realm.

> till I entered God's Sanctuary
> and understood their fate.

The poet has exited from the reality of this world and entered into another space that provides a new perspective of what is true. Here one sees existence differently: in the world out there, the pious can feel displaced, exiled, overwhelmed, but here, in the sanctuary, one feels assured of a different truth. Entering God's temple, the space where one comes closest to God, all understandings of life are transformed.

A truth stands beyond the daily world we encounter. Viewing the world from that perspective, one sees that wealth and power are superficial and transitory, that another story can be told—the truths of the heart. There is an experience of the world that can be quite different than the one sustained by the physical and material world.

> Though my body and heart fail,
> God is my heart's fortress, my portion forever.

The physical heart may fail, the body may give out, but the secret of life is that the heart provides an entree to another reality—the presence of God. This other world may be found even in moments of doubt, even when the pious despair, even when life seems oppressive, still—

> You held my right hand;
> You guided me by Your counsel.

You continued to be with me even as I questioned, you continued to speak to me in my heart of hearts even while all I could see was the power and wealth that others had amassed. You allowed me to see that honor could mean something quite different from the rewards offered by society.

> You place them amidst mirages;
> You make them fall through blandishments.
>
> How suddenly are they ruined,
> wholly swept away, ended through confusion.

They will pass. Their world, which seems so real, will ultimately prove to be fleeting. What is accepted as incontrovertible truth today proves, in time, to be ephemeral. Theirs is the dream. The inner truth, which seems to others the world of fantasy, flimsy reverie, is in fact the true reality.

> As for me, nearness to God is good;
> I have made the Lord, Adonai, my refuge,
> to recount all Your works.

I choose to live in a different realm. I experience the religious life as good. I will tell a different story: I will recount Your works.

Now that is certainly a strange outcome, since God's works are absent, not visible, which is, after all, the point of the extended argument that constitutes the first part of the poem. The conclusion makes sense only if we understand the works mentioned here as the work of the heart. No "objective" works of God would prove the reality of the religious life. The poet seems to be arguing that we miss the point of the religious life if we look outside of the heart for God. It is the inner sense of the "nearness to God," the felt presence of God in one's heart, that constitutes the ultimate good. Alone, in my home, I can contemplate God's promise, I can experience my life as filled with possibility, an opening to the future; I can understand my life as filled with blessing, and I can realize how I myself might be a blessing. The story that needs to be told by the pious is not what material goods have been afforded by the relationship with God, but what inner vision God has provided.

> Though my body and heart fail,
> God is my heart's fortress, my portion forever.

An identity is established between going into the sanctuary and entering the chambers of one's heart. In fact, Martin Buber, in commenting on this psalm, points out that the key word *heart* is one of the repetitive elements in this poem. It represents the inner life that stands opposed to the outer reality occupied by the world of power and wealth. The heart is a different realm; its rule is other than the forces at work in the world outside. Entering the sanctuary, the poet moves inward and discovers the life of her own heart. The sanctuary is an opening to an inner reality where the power displayed by the rulers, by the advantaged, is no longer relevant; the world of apparent abundance is not the true reality. The physical body cultivated by the wealthy looks good, but for the human it is the innerly vision that opens us to unseen, but ultimately significant, realms.

Interestingly, William Sidney's seventeenth-century rendering of this psalm captures precisely this understanding.

> And my unworthy lips, inspired with thy grace,
> Shall thus forespeak thy secret works in sight of Adam's race.[1]

What can be announced by the poet is God's "secret works" because that is the truth of God's presence that the author has experienced. God's real works are always hidden.

> As for me, nearness to God is good;
> I have made the Lord, Adonai, my refuge,
> to recount all Your works.

The poet has laid two realities side by side. The first is the triumph of a material world, a realm described only by what one can see: a self-satisfied world of seeming success and power, a world of "beautiful people," a sphere circumscribing injustice and corruption. The other reality is revealed in the sanctuary; it is touched by God's presence; its ways are of truth and justice and love; its resonances can be found in the secret recesses of the heart. It is hidden, its reality hardly tangible, but it describes an adamantine truth.

How does anyone know which perspective is reality, which fantasy? The fact is that each person takes a stand on one side of this question or the other—and each person sees the other side as the realm of fantasy. The two perspectives constitute different visions of life, and ultimately one cannot be proven and the other disproved but one chooses one way or the other. I, announces the poet, take my stand (after having been tempted by another

---

1. Wieder, *The Poets' Book of Psalms*.

way of being) with the way of holiness, and in adopting that stance, I have found validation beyond my imagining in hidden daily miracles, subtle blessings, inner rewards of my impulse to do what is good. The first word the poet speaks in the poem is *I* and the last sentence begins with *I*. All I can do is take my stand and go on:

> to recount all Your works.

Just as the poem begins with a sentence fragment, it now ends with one. The poem began with a cliché, "Surely good to Israel, God to the clear hearted," and now it ends with "to recount all Your works." In the course of these two fragments we have come to understand goodness in a very different and new way because the heart has taken on different meaning. God comes to the clear hearted. God enters the heart—that is the goodness that has been promised and spoken about of old. The "works" that will be spoken of are these works of the heart. The entire poem has subverted any claim to objective works of God toward which the pious can point. The world does not reflect God's rule; instead what the poet can describe is a presence that she has found in the center of her heart; all there is, all that can exist out there in the world, is the telling.

The medieval Jewish commentator Rashi interprets the word "works" as "message"—i.e., divine inspiration. The work of God is the writing of the poem, which is then recited as a traditional psalm. In Rashi's reading, the poet is saying, I am left with the telling of the story of my finding You, God, which I understand is Your work. My speech of faithfulness is the work of Your hand and my entree to You. The objective evidence the poet can offer of God's presence is the poem itself.

The poet's message regarding the life of faith is that the reality that stands over against the religious argument is powerful, but in the end there is a life of the heart that material prosperity can never describe. It is there that eternity is touched. Everything else is finite, transient. I continue to tell Your story, and in the telling, sense more and more of Your presence. All evidence to the contrary, I continue to believe because of the reality of my heart's imaginings. Your whispering presence is what is true. It is only the matters of the heart that are lasting. Of this I shall speak, says the poet, and the reader of the poem in repeating the words may find a whisper of this idea in his or her own heart.

11

Psalm 39

Despair and Response

WE HAVE EXAMINED PERSONAL suffering and exile as themes of complaint. Similarly, we have seen psalmists voice outrage at injustice, both as an expression of personal experience and as they view it dominating society at large. There is also another theme that appears as a source of complaint in psalms: the human condition itself. Psalmists will remark on the brevity of life, at how passing existence seems to be. To be human is to be subject to death, and as one grows older the reality of one's own finitude becomes more and more striking. Contemplation of death can give rise to a sense of the futility of human activity. We die, and do not see the consequences of our lives. It is easy to imagine that all we have built up is washed away and disappears like our physical bodies. We have no control over what happens after we're gone.

And death can come at any time. There is an old German adage: *Man tracht und Gott lacht.* (Humans plan, God laughs.) Death makes light of the seriousness with which we take our lives, the energy we expend on building our future. Our lives are composed of many plans for the future, but death makes a mockery of our agenda.

Everything we accomplish has the air of imperfection and impermanence about it. Weighed against the perfection of God and the infinite power of the Creator, our acts and deeds add up to little. Whatever we create will be buried by the sands of the desert and the seas of time and the universe goes on. We are an inconsequential speck in the cosmos. This sense of futility animates the author of one of the most problematic, cynical, and gloomy books of the Bible—Ecclesiastes. These questions are the themes of the next two psalms we examine and they go to the heart of human angst.

The opening of Psalm 39 is most reminiscent of Ecclesiastes: life is futile. In fact, the same word, *hevel* ("futile"), which opens the book of Ecclesiastes is used here at the culmination of the argument in verse seven. The struggle with human finitude is the theme of this psalm—its question is clear, its final resolution a subject of scholarly debate. I offer one possible translation here, but in discussing this psalm I will also mention other proposed endings that give it a quite different flavor.

PSALM 39

1   *Of the conductor—for Jeduthan—A Davidic Psalm*

2   I said that I would watch my ways
    lest I sin with my tongue—
    I would watch my mouth, muzzle it,
    while evil stands opposite me.

3   I was silent, dumb
    —utterly quiet—
    but my pain intensified.

4   Inside, my heart boiled;
    my groans were like burning flames;
    so I spoke out.

5   God would You tell me when my life will end?
    What is the measure of my days?
    Then I will truly know how finite I am.

6   You made my days only handbreadths long,
    the span of my life is as nothing before You,
    for isn't everything—every standing human being—just a passing
        breath?   *Selah*

7   For though mortals seem to walk in the image of God,
    still their speech is futile:
    they amass things but do not know who will gather them up.

8   And now, what can I look forward to, God?
    My hope lies with You.

9   Save me from all my transgressions,
    don't make me feel shame like a fool.

10   I would be silent,
      I will not open my mouth,
      for my fate is Your doing.

11   Take away Your plague from me;
      the attacks of Your hands would make me perish.

12   As reproach for sinning You chastise people,
      melting away their most precious possessions,
      for aren't all human beings just a passing breath? *Selah*

13   Hear my prayer, God, and redeem me,
      listen to my tears,
      do not be still,
      for in Your realm I am a stranger,
      a resident alien like all my ancestors.

14   Delight in me and I will be strengthened,
      before I die and am no more.

This is a difficult poem, and it helps to try to divide the stanzas. There are three parts to this poem: first, the introductory verses (verses 1–3) where the poet describes the effort to keep silent. Second, the middle section (verses 4–7), when finally what can no longer be held in is spoken, and the poet asks the questions, "How long will I live?" What will my life add up to? And last, the ending (verses 8–14), where doubt and complaint are turned into prayer. Each shift constitutes a remarkable turning.

The burning quality of the questioning—in an image the author himself uses—is described in graphic terms: I would muzzle my mouth. The silence is meant as an act of piety: I will not speak because it will be understood by God's enemies as a failure of faith. What is internal and unexpressed is not sinful, rather to utter the complaint is to give fuel to sinners. Speech is an act; uttered complaint, an argument against God. Yet it is animals that are muzzled, and the human in closing off the possibility of speech is reduced to animality. Piety seemingly demands a loss of the fullness of being human.

> I was silent, dumb,
> —utterly quiet—
> but my pain intensified.

Three different synonyms for silence are used, ending with the judgment that the price of silence is overwhelming pain. Human beings ought not to have to suffer this intense pain as the price of faithfulness.

> Inside, my heart boiled;
> my groans were like burning flames;
> so I spoke out.

The speech cannot be contained; it burns. The poet must use his tongue for what it was meant. God must listen. The mouth that was stopped up now flows with words, and thoughts burst forth. Although the first question out of the author's mouth is not a particularly heretical one—what will be the length of my life?—as the questioning of God continues, it becomes clear that what is really at stake is the challenging of the very meaning of life and that question constitutes a doubting of the wisdom of God's creation.

> God, would You tell me when my life will end?
> What is the measure of my days?
> Then I will truly know how finite I am.

Seemingly, the most human of questions pours out: How long do I have to live? Don't let my future be open ended, unknown; tell me what I can plan for. Why make my days a constant facing of the irrational?

But the author is not simply posing an innocent question for which an answer is requested; any answer will be the source of a complaint: die at fifty, eighty—it all goes so fast; life is soon over, whatever the number, I would have to face how finite I am.

> You made my days only handbreadths long,
> the span of my life is as nothing before You,
> for isn't everything—every standing human being—just a passing
> breath?

Here is the real source of anguish: it doesn't matter how long we live; in the end, human life adds up to nothing. We may glorify our accomplishments, but the fact of our death flies in the face of their worth.

> For, though mortals seem to walk in the image of God,
> still their speech is futile,
> they amass things but do not know who will gather them up.

We act, but the consequences of our deeds will be unknown to us, another generation will make something quite different of what we have built.

The New Jewish Publication Society Translation translates the first part of the verse as: "humanity walks about as a mere shadow." The Hebrew word *tzelem* means "form" and contains within it the word *tzel,* meaning "shadow," but it is most significantly used in Genesis where human beings are created in the *tzelem* (the very "image") of God. The verse takes on greater significance if it is read as an ironic statement referencing Genesis: Yes, you say that we are created in Your very image, but though we have a certain power of mastery, we remain finite, and death laughs at all that we have amassed, all that we have produced. The human, unlike the animal, is supposed to reflect the image of God, yet our fate is ultimately no different from that of any animal on earth. We are inconsequential, only a cipher, an anonymous link in a biological chain.

The reason for the psalmist's original silence is now quite clear. Once the expression of pain begins, it leads to heretical places. The psalmist questions the very meaning of life: human existence has no purpose. God's existence is not denied; the opposite is the case: the affirmation of God's existence and power makes us realize how paltry and finite our own lives are.

After the psalmist expresses these heretical rumblings, something quite different overtakes the psalmist. The author begins with the phrase, "And now . . ." Now that I've expressed my secret resentments, now that I have poured out my fears and complaints . . . "and now . . . ," what am I left with? I am left facing You God. I've stripped away all pretense, understood that my possessions, my labor, add up to nothing. "And now?"

> And now, what can I look forward to, God?
> My hope lies with You.

All there is for me is Your presence, Your blessing. Be with me, if for a moment, for that moment would count as an eternity as nothing else can be. Human striving may mean nothing. I cannot bless my own handiwork, but if you would see significance in my existence, then I would know that my own sense of futility could be overcome.

This thought makes the psalmist aware of how he might have separated himself from God. If the ultimate purpose of life is to be with God, then what of the sins, the mistakes, the misguided turnings of my life that have turned me from You?

> Save me from all my transgressions,
> don't make me feel shame like a fool.

> Take away Your plague from me;
> the attacks of Your hands would make me perish.

Ultimately, I face You. Don't make me pay for all my human error. I said to You, I am finite; recognize that in me. Let me turn to You in my incompleteness. Bless me even in my finitude.

Complaint has turned to prayer. The psalmist himself names his speech in that way, turning to God and pleading, "Hear my prayer." Prayer for the psalmist is a turning to God with an expression of regret issuing in a plea not to be turned away from God's presence; acceptance of my human failing, forgiveness on Your part, would bring a purity of being that would allow me to stand in Your presence.

> Hear my prayer, God, and redeem me;
> listen to my tears;
> do not be still,
> for in Your realm I am a stranger,
> a resident alien like all my ancestors.

I accept You and the world You have created. In fact, it is in this acceptance that I discover who I am: a finite human being, a person who can easily take wrong turns, ultimately powerless, owning nothing, a stranger everywhere, to You, to myself, lost. All life is in Your hands. Nothing else matters save Your forgiveness, Your blessing.

> I would be silent.
> I will not open my mouth,
> for my fate is Your doing.

"I would be silent"—here we have an expression of silence, echoing the beginning of the poem. In the beginning, the poet found it impossible to keep silent; in fact, enforced silence only heated up his anger, made his condition even more intolerable. But now we have the silence that comes after speech, the silence that waits for a reply. One waits for the God who blesses, the one who redeems, the one who gives ultimate meaning to the few moments that we have here on earth.

In sum, the poet understands that he has moved from complaint to prayer and names his speech a prayer. He understands the human condition, his own, and that of all generations who have preceded him as that of being not quite at home here on earth. We all only pass through; we all are strangers here on earth. We do not have title to life; we all receive it as a gift, not as a right. We are not citizens who can make demands of life, only guests on earth.

But there is this: God loves the stranger. That, of course, is the central story of the Hebrew Bible: You were once strangers in the land of Egypt, and God took you out of there, because God listens to the tears of the oppressed. Your ancestor was Abraham, the Hebrew—the one who came from beyond the river, the man who could only follow God by leaving home, by learning how to live as a stranger amid foreign peoples.

Therefore, in describing himself as a resident alien, the psalmist is expressing a dual thought: the human is always a dweller in a strange land, our feelings of being at home, of owning our possessions, are illusions. We are always just passing through life. The twists and turns of life so easily remove our sense of control of our own destinies. And this: it is only when we recognize our contingency that we have a special claim on God, for God turns to the poor and disenfranchised. God loves us when we appear before God naked, with no masks, no possessions to hide behind.

This may be a difficult religious perspective to take. We want our own merit to count for something; we want to believe in our worth; we want to feel that the products of our lives—our work, our loves—have some intrinsic value. To recognize that our lives are brief and that all we do adds up to less than little seems inhuman, unjust. The poet turns to God with a plea for forgiveness. Only You can see that the ultimate intent was good and that the mistakes of my life were a result of the fact that I am all too human. Recognize me for what I am, Your creation, and bless me in my incompleteness. What the poet seems to discover is that it is only when we recognize ourselves as caught in our own finitude that the complete turning to God can take place.

> Delight in me and I will be strengthened,
> before I die and am no more.

What I can have, which can make it all worthwhile, is a time of knowing that you are pleased with me. Were I to know that who I am, what I do, indeed gives you joy, then I would overcome my sense of smallness. For one moment I would find happiness, and that one moment of blessing would make my life feel whole.

This request goes beyond some that we have met previously in psalms. For instance, in Psalm 27 where the psalmist asks for only one thing: to see God in the land of the living. The request to see God, to be with God, is different than the plea uttered here, which is essentially a prayer for God to see me, for God to recognize me as a being of worth, for the infinite to see value in the work of the finite, for the God who is perfect to accept the product of imperfect hands, and, most extraordinary of all in this rendering, for God to "delight" in the psalmist.

In fact, the Hebrew here is difficult. Not uncommonly, translators offer an interpretation that is the very opposite of the one offered here. I have translated the Hebrew verb *hashah* as "delight," interpreting it as a verbal form of the common Hebrew noun *sha-a-shua*—"that which is enjoyed" (in modern Hebrew, "plaything"). It has also been translated as "remove" or "raise up," which is the way most of the ancient commentators understood it. If that is the case, what the poet may be asking is that sin be removed. But more recently some scholars have argued that the root verb means "to see" or "to gaze." Thus the contemporary JPS translation reads, "Look away from me . . ." Similarly, the Anchor Bible volume has, "Turn your gaze from me . . ."[1]

This is a quite extraordinary view expressed nowhere else in the book of Psalms: that my salvation will come, not in God's looking at me, but in God's looking away from me. Psalmists constantly express the wish to be in the presence of God. In fact, God's hiding God's face (i.e., the lack of God's presence) is most often seen as the source of despair. This psalmist would ask God to leave off, as if to say, it is only when the Infinite One looks away, is not present, judgmental, overbearing, that human life makes sense. For it is only then when God does not set the standard of judgment, that we can live with human imperfection and make some sense of our lives.

Indeed, that is what Job feels. Parts of both chapter 7 and chapter 10 of the book of Job exhibit remarkable linguistic parallels to our psalm. In some moments, Job sees God as an enemy, or as an "other" who can hardly understand and sympathize with the human condition:

1. Even if we accept the meaning of *hashah* as related to gaze, the following alternate translation might be offered, which would accord with my reading of this psalm:

> Fill your gaze with me and I will be delighted . . .

There is some disagreement about the next word, the Hebrew *avligah*, which all the medievals translate as "strengthened" and which some contemporary scholars translate as "diverted" or "delighted." If we accept the latter meaning of the word, it might make sense to combine it with my interpretation of "*hashah*" and thus the verse may read:

> Delight in me and I will be happy . . .

More recently, some have translated the word as "catch my breath," for example, Alter, *The Book of Psalms*.

> Do You have eyes of flesh?
> Do You see as humans do?
> Are Your days like those of men and women?
> Are the years of Your life like the days of people? (Job 10:4)

In these moments, Job sees God's infinity as overwhelming human time. God's perfection and timelessness create an abyss between divine and human being. The two live in different spheres, and there is no possibility of empathy on God's part—no understanding of the frustration of our humanity, our limitations, our imperfection. And so Job can demand that God go away, leave him alone, for God can never be truly empathic.

In chapter 7, in a series of verses that are a play on psalms, Job remarks:

> Why can't you leave (*tisheh*) me alone . . .

(or it may be more literally translated "Why don't You remove yourself from me?"). The same letters of the verb occur in Job as occur here as an end to Psalm 39. Many scholars argue that the author of Job must have known our psalm, or that the two authors lived at the same time. Many read our psalm in light of Job and translate this last line accordingly. For instance, the contemporary translator Robert Alter offers the following:

> Look away from me, that I may catch my breath[2]
> before I depart and am not.

I believe that it could well be that the author of the book of Job knew our psalm and played on its language, turning the message of our psalm on its head. The linguistic parallels are so strong that it seems probable that the two passages are related. That is what has impelled many scholars to feel that our psalmist is verbalizing similar thoughts. We know that Job often ironically quotes other parts of the Bible or twists a verse so that it is given new, almost heretical, meaning, and this too may be such an instance.

But our poet expresses a different mood than does the author of the book of Job. Job despairs of God; the author of Psalm 39 still hopes for a relationship with God. Job refuses to accept his sinfulness as a cause for his suffering; our psalmist believes that in the moment of regret, in the recognition of human imperfection, there can be a turning toward God and a return to God's presence. Therefore, while Job can only experience life as all too short—the grave opens up before him—the author of Psalm 39 feels

---

2. See the previous note as to Alter's translation as "catch my breath."

that one moment of feeling accepted by God can make all of life worth it. Indeed, another overtone of the word *hashah* is the Hebrew *yeshuah* ("victory"). To be included within God's vision is to be part of God's victorious entry into the world. Here too I would think that if we take the meaning of the verb to be "look away," it should not be understood as a request that God look away from the poet, but that God look away from the poet's transgressions. I have translated this verse:

> Delight in me and I will be strengthened,
> before I die and am no more.

But if the verb is understood with the related meaning of triumph, it might be put this way:

> Let me be seen as a part of Your triumph and I will be strengthened
> before I die and am no more.

In this rendition, the poet is saying, "If I only knew that I was a part of Your triumph, that I am part of Your victory in the world, then all would be well; my life would be justified." What the poet is then asking for is to see his life as part of the process of redemption. In either of my readings, in the poet's mind, it is God's standing in relation to us, of our being assured that our lives are part of a larger world of meaning, that can offer a moment of redemption.

The poet's questions can easily be seen as our questions as well. Our lives, too, can feel too short, and we may be struck by the futility of what we attempt to do, what we attempt to build. We may look at our grown children and wonder where the years have gone. We may leave a job, look over our shoulder and find that a successor undoes everything we have put in place. We may try to comfort a friend or loved one only to end up feeling that our efforts were bumbling, that we only increased the pain. We may try ourselves to be creators and be struck by how amateurish our handiwork is. Everything we do can seem paltry, passing. Life can feel all too short, burdensome, full of disappointment, hardly worth the while.

Reading Psalm 39, we might begin to appreciate how much a moment of grace, a moment of feeling that our faults are forgiven and that God delights in us, can mean. To achieve such a moment, I would give up all that is petty and superficial—my jealousies, my game playing, my need to appear fashionable, to be pleasing to others. Instead, I would be able to feel worthwhile in and of myself, not for any of my accomplishments but for whom I've become, how I enter a day, greet the morning. In such a moment I would feel that I in my uniqueness am blessed by God, that the creator has given me life as a gift because God entrusted me with a unique personality, an individual breath. I would truly experience myself as in the image of God. I would need nothing more than this sense to experience delight in life. In my moment of turning, God would welcome me. Such a moment would be sufficient for the fulfillment of my life—my prayer would be answered.

Would that it would happen to this stranger.

12

Psalm 90

Time and Eternity

PSALM 39 POSES A dilemma about time: God's time, eternity, may leave no place for the human being—the thought of eternity overwhelms human finitude. We are fragile, finite, imperfect; our works are paltry; is the only standard of judgment to be perfection, divine perfection? Is there nothing we do that is significant, that has permanence? These questions, which troubled the author of Psalm 39, are at the forefront of concern for the author of Psalm 90 as well. But where the resolution of Psalm 39 is a matter of some debate, the point of Psalm 90 is clear. This psalm, even more emphatically than the one we just read, returns us to the human condition, and calls down a blessing on our earthly, fleeting, imperfect handiwork—human creation.

PSALM 90

1 A prayer of Moses, the man of God.
  O lord, You have been our refuge in every generation.

2 Before the mountains were born,
  before You formed the earth and the world,
  forever and ever, You are God.

3 You return human beings to dust,
  as You said, "Return, children of Adam!"

4   For in Your sight a thousand years
are but a passing yesterday,
a watch in the night—

5   "They will be engulfed by sleep."
Each morning they are like constantly changing grass;

6   in the morning it flourishes anew;
at evening, it withers and dries up.

7   So we are consumed by Your anger,
terror-struck by Your fury.

8   You set our transgressions before You,
our secrets revealed by the light of Your face.

9   For all our days, we face Your wrath;
our years pass as quickly as a sigh.

10   The span of our life is seventy years,
or given strength, eighty years
and most of them are filled with travail and sorrow.
They pass speedily, and we disappear.

11   Who can know the strength of Your anger?
Your wrath matches the fear of You.

12   Teach us to count our days rightly,
that we may obtain a wise heart.

13   Return, Adonai! How long will it take?
Comfort Your servants.

14   In the morning, satisfy us with Your love
that we may sing with joy all of our days.

15   Give us happiness equal to the days of our affliction,
the years we have seen misfortune.

16   Let Your deeds be seen by Your servants,
Your glory by their children.

17   May the grace of the lord, our God, be upon us;
and establish the work of our hands upon us—
the work of our hands—establish it!

At the heart of Psalm 90, a meditation on time's passing, is the apprehension of death, the knowledge that our time is to be over, that our individual fate is oblivion.

The confrontation with time is a human concern, but not a concern of a timeless God. We count minutes, tear off passing days from the calendar, observe everything as fleeting. It is we who are overcome with the fear of death. This is the "gift" of our self-consciousness. God's time is eternity. God was before all there is and will be after there is an end.

The first words of the psalm (I will deal with the ascription to Moses, verse 1, at the end) entail an assurance: God is our refuge, our home. We have seen by now that many psalms begin with a simple statement of faith. Sometimes these statements can feel like a slogan or a cliché, a pious platitude that was part of common religious parlance. It is a statement that sounds right, God is our refuge, yet what does it truly mean? In what sense is God a refuge? Am I truly protected from the assaults of the world through my faith? Is not my relationship with God itself troubling? As it turns out, it is in fact this pious assertion that the psalmist will see as problematic, for it will evoke for the supplicant the incredible gulf between the human and the divine. Rather than offering refuge, the idea of God will raise for the psalmist the central anxieties of human existence.

> O lord, You have been our refuge in every generation.

We are wanderers over the face of the earth. We have no real ancestral home. The Hebrew word *ma-on*, translated here as "refuge," is sometimes used in the Bible to refer to an animal's lair, the hidden place in the forest where a lion, for instance, might slink back after having foraged near civilization, or satiated itself with its prey. God is that hidden place we have come from and go back to in order to find succor.

But this opening thought, seemingly filled with assurance, lays bare underlying anxieties. The verse continues with the emphasis on the succession of generations, the return to God that has been true of every generation; but this succession of generations carries with it the knowledge of our own dying. God is with us and with our children and with the generation beyond that. The Creator was there at the beginning of time, and God will be present long after our passing. We may spend time here on earth (indeed it is God who has placed us here), but God has also set in motion an inevitable rule: our time must come to an end. God will reign forever, and we will pass from the scene; others will rise in importance, and in time we will be forgotten. They will find God their refuge, but we will be long gone.

Note that at the very opening of the psalm and at its conclusion God is not addressed by a personal name or by the second-person preposition but by the formal title, *Lord*.[1] Only once in the poem is the personal name

---

1. The King James Version translated the personal name of God, *Yod-Heh-Vav-Heh*,

of God used: in verse 12 when God is directly addressed in prayer. This is a poem in which the author is overwhelmed by the difference between the human and the divine. Almost the entire poem carries the sense that God is lord and master, and that we are insignificant pawns in the larger unfolding of history.

> Before the mountains were born,
> before You formed the earth and the world,
> forever and ever, You are God.

God is timeless, existing before creation and living after all is gone.

> You return human beings to dust,
> as You said, "Return, children of Adam!"

The psalmist evokes the magnificent language of the creation, but then brings to mind the primal story of the human expulsion from the Garden. The creator God who formed us also ensured our dying. The verb *return*, used twice here, is the same as that describing the curse on Adam in Genesis 3:19:

> "By the sweat of your brow you shall eat bread
> till you *return* to the earth,
> for it is from there you came,
> and to dust you shall *return*." (adapted from NJPS)

Thus the reference to human beings as "the descendants of Adam," though a standard Hebrew phrase for humanity, is not incidental to the message of the psalmist. Adam sinned and was chased from the Garden; the fruit of the tree of life was forever foreclosed to the first human beings—and to their successors. Your time, God, is forever; ours is but a lifetime—this was our curse from the very beginning. And our limited lifespan is a constant reminder to us of our imperfection, our finitude.

This contrast between human and divine time is emphasized in the next two verses of Psalm 90:

> For in Your sight a thousand years
> are but a passing yesterday,
> a watch in the night—
> "They will be engulfed by sleep."

---

as "Lord," but here the personal name does not appear. Instead the actual Hebrew word for "master" or "lord" appears. To differentiate the two, I have spelled *lord* in the translation of this psalm with a lower-case initial letter.

> Each morning they are like constantly changing grass;
> in the morning it flourishes anew;
> at evening, it withers and dries up.

The difference between divine time and human time could not be stated more sharply. A millennium, which seems so vast to us, is only a day from the point of view of the cosmos. In our terms we might say that the vastness of the universe's time, measured in billions of years, overwhelms the significance of our days. Truly, a light-year, less than the distance of one galaxy to the next, is a mathematical formula but is beyond our imagining. We think so much of ourselves, we make so much of our time, yet our lives are but brief passing moments. Measured against the universe we are dwarfed into insignificance. In biblical times, there were three watches in the night; a watch was just four hours. That is what our lives must seem like in God's eyes—so brief. Death is inevitable, and contemplating its approach, we are always struck by how short our lives are.

Life is short, and what little time we have is squandered, or worse, it is spent damaging our inheritance. Most of our time is not spent well, and when the moment passes we realize how insubstantial our entertainments have been. As we look at our motives, we feel how petty our behavior and concerns: how our lives are ruled by competition and jealousy, how frequently we've acted as though earning more money, buying the right clothing, displaying more wealth, exercising petty power, displaying sexual prowess will make us seem more worthy even in our eyes, if not in the eyes of our friends and rivals. We live but seventy years and if lucky eighty, (these days we may live till ninety, but do those added ten years, so wished for, really make a difference?) Our years are mostly years of "travail and sorrow. They pass speedily, and we disappear."

The consciousness of the brevity and trouble of our lives is a continuous replaying of the expulsion from the garden: the punishment pronounced to Adam was first of all the curse of hard work for little reward, and second, mortality, the knowledge that dreams always face the mockery of death. And so the psalmist meditates on God's anger—on the waste we have made of creation, on the constant human repetition of sinning, and on the brevity of our lives.

> So we are consumed by Your anger,
> terror-struck by Your fury.

> You set our transgressions before You,
> our secrets revealed by the light of Your face.
>
> For all our days, we face Your wrath;
> our years pass as quickly as a sigh.
>
> The span of our life is seventy years,
> or given strength, eighty years,
> and most of them are filled with travail and sorrow.
> They pass speedily, and we disappear.

These are human truths, learned anew in every generation: much of our life is troubled, wracked by feelings of dissatisfaction. We are imperfect and mortal. Our inner lives and outer behavior are filled with little sins: shaded truths, jealousies, petty betrayals. And many times with greater transgressions as well. We are constantly tempted and never faultless. We may be aware of our failures and failings or not, but they are surely there.

But the psalmist does not want to end there; creation is also the story of a gift, God's gift. We also have the ability to create, we have a capacity for generosity, and we can reflect on our lives and grow. And so another religious truth is now placed alongside the first. The psalmist turns and prays:

> Teach us to count our days rightly,
> that we may obtain a wise heart.

Instead of the years of our short lifetime, we are asked to contemplate a single day and the poet pleads: Grant us enlightenment to make this day count. May human time matter. May what is given to us, a day, today, be valued. May what I do today be worthwhile even if for a moment.

To be human is to be imperfect. Falling short of the ideal is the inevitable fate of every person's life. Our acts can never match the divine image. So if the separation between the human and God is based on our knowledge of our imperfection, then we will never meet the divine and never measure up to divine expectation. But God can bless the work of our hands (though it is never perfect), can acknowledge it as a proper offering, can receive the proffered gift of our torn hearts. That acceptance would constitute a divine forgiveness of our finite imperfection. In that moment of acceptance, the gulf between the human and the divine would be overcome. The lord of all the universe would meet human being.

And so the psalmist prays that the distance between God and creation may be overcome.

> Return, Adonai! How long will it take?
> Comfort Your servants.

Do we have to wait for eternity to bridge the abyss between God and human beings? Can't divine grace be manifest in human time? Can't God reach into the sphere of human imperfection? Provocatively, the psalmist uses the word "return" as pertaining to God. God has cursed the human with the words, "return to the earth," but God's own "return to earth" will issue in redemption (the Hebrew uses the same exact word in both cases). God's return to earth will bring blessing—will give human time significance; it will overcome the expulsion from the garden, the exile from God's presence. God's contemporary blessing will overcome God's original curse. Here finally, God is addressed with God's personal name: *Yod, Heh, Vav, Heh.* The poet seeks God's comfort and God's love and kindness, which is withheld when God judges us and reminds us of our mortality. In praying to God and calling upon God with the divine personal name, the poet is evoking God's beneficence, which can break through the distance between the human and God.

> In the morning, satisfy us with Your love
> that we may sing with joy all of our days.

The poet uses the same word *boqer* ("morning") that he used earlier to describe the grass that emerges in the morning and dries up by evening. It is as if to say, satisfy us within the bounds of human time. If our lives are to be but a day in your sight, then enter into our reality, be with us at the dawn. The probable etymology of the Hebrew word *boqer* ("morning") is the verb "to split"—the dawn *splits* the darkness of the night: God, enter into our gloom, split it apart, allow us to see the light, if only for a day, if not also for the morrow.

> May the grace of the lord, our God, be upon us;
> and establish the work of our hands upon us—
> the work of our hands—establish it!

An opposition arises between chronological time, which is fleeting (in which the ticking of the second hand is the witness to finitude), and eternity, transcendent timelessness. That which is meaningful is lasting (i.e., transcends the ravages of time), yet all that is human is subject to decay, is a victim of time's passing. The secret of religious existence is to connect the two kinds of time.

In fact, these verses point to a reversal that has taken place in the poem. Literary scholars of the Bible speak of a chiastic structure: half an *x* (the Greek letter *chi* forms an *x*) frequently encountered in the Bible. Opening thoughts and closing ones match each other, as do second lines and penultimate lines. The opening of the poem begins with God having created the world, and the closing calls down a blessing on our own creation. The second thought is about God's curse to Adam saying that Adam will "return" to the dust, and the penultimate thought asks God to "return to us." The poem in its beginning talks of the human's brief life, and in the second part the poet asks us to "number our days." Finally, at first the poet talks of God's anger at our sinfulness, and in the second half the poet pleads that God's wrath not be overwhelming.

And so as the psalmist comes to the end, the psalmist asks that human creation have meaning alongside divine creation mentioned at the beginning, and prays: grant to our fleeting human efforts a measure of permanence, a touch of divinity. Let human activity parallel divine activity. If the human is created in the image of God and has been impelled by God to enter into earthly existence, as Genesis 1 argues, then it must be possible to think of the transitory human artifact as having the possibility of containing within it a measure of timelessness, a touch of the divine.

What is meant by "the work of our hands," that for which we seek blessing? In an act of love, in a tragic moment when comfort is offered, in the assertion of human dignity for those who have been deprived of privilege, in human imagining and creation, heaven and earth can meet. In that moment, the human transitory act can take on eternal significance.

I realize that my translation of the second line of this last verse—"establish the work of our hands upon us"—is somewhat awkward and the meaning may not be immediately obvious. I did not want to lose the force of the Hebrew preposition. The exact same word is used in the Hebrew in the first and second lines of this last verse: *aleinu*, translated here as "upon us." I understand this usage as an object of the verb "establish," as an expression of the wish that we may be the starting point of something that has continuity, just as God's power is continuous in time, reaching from one generation to another, so may we. In fact, that is what it would signify for something to be established—that it would have meaning beyond this time, this generation. God can bless this creation of mine, this act, so that it has a measure of the divine and is not immediately subject to human finitude, so that another generation finds it significant, takes it on as a teaching.

What gives Psalm 90 power is the overwhelming consciousness of the finite nature of human time. How fleeting and passing is our time on earth! We are like grass growing in the desert: a sudden rain comes and the grass springs to life. The next day, the sun beats down again and everything dries up.

Yet even the desert contains a wonderful and mysterious continuity of life. And Psalm 90 begins and ends with this remark on life bridging generations and maintaining continuity despite the transitory nature of individual existence. The grass sprouting for a day is a link in the chain of the continuous life the desert nourishes. For one day it may flower and produce a seed that will flourish in a future time that this original flower will never see. But it is the work of that one day which is the carrier of the continuity of life. So too with the human: our flourishing may be blessed so that it births something in a time we will not ourselves experience.

We can now see that the psalm's beginning is wonderfully ironic:

O lord, You have been our refuge in every generation.

The use of the word "generation" rather than "time" or any other synonym is deliberate. Generational change is in fact both the problem and the solution. The passing of the generations is the anxiety that initiates the poet's speech. Birth is a signal of death, the coming of a new generation signals the passing of another. Yet it is through intergenerational transmission that the overcoming of time can be achieved, that something more lasting than one's own lifetime is created. What can be most enduring in that process of intergenerational transmission is the work of our hands that helps establish God's kingdom—the teaching and establishment of words and work that speak justice, truth, and love that have lasting value.

When we act with love and care, when the work of our hands fulfills a dream consonant with divine purpose, then another generation might hear the divine calling from within as well. The lasting quality of what we accomplish might not be immediately obvious, but over the course of thousands of years (i.e., God's time) it becomes evident. Jeremiah may have been mocked during his own life, but his teaching has effected countless generations; we still read the words of this psalm for succor, though it was written thousands of years ago. (In certain moments we can even hear the weeping of many generations as they read this psalm.) My grandmother, who took her newborn son home from the hospital and cared daily for him, despite his grave condition at birth and the doctor's prediction of his imminent death, saved my father and so gave me life, and life to my children. Seen or unseen, remembered by others or not, acts can gain significance by being a part of God's accounting. There is then an alternative system of meaning, one which transforms the view of our everyday struggle for existence into transcendent purpose, and places our acts within a continuous stream of life.

As at the beginning, so at the end, the poet alludes to this intergenerational transmission:

> Let Your deeds be seen by Your servants,
> Your glory by their children.

God's appearance, which is timeless, has the power to overcome the generational divide. When our own works are attached to this larger vision, they can be lasting: they can be seen both by one generation and the next. Chronological time can collapse, and eternity open before us.

> May the grace of the Lord, our God, be upon us;
> and establish the work of our hands upon us—
> the work of our hands—establish it!

The One who is before creation, the Creator, is the only one who can affirm that our creation will be transcendent. Our time is touched by timelessness when it comes close to the original work of God's hand and the ravages of time are overcome. May God bless the work of our hands so that we too may be considered creators.

One of the key wordplays at work in the psalm is "return." In the poem, the word is first spoken by God to human beings, and is a sentence of death. At the end of the poem the human, the poet, utters the word as a prayer directed toward God. The word *shuva* ("return") is used throughout prophetic literature for the turning of the human toward God and is frequently translated into English as "repent." It is repentance, the turning of the human toward divine purpose, that has the power to turn the divine toward the human. The repentance of our imperfection—the prayer at the heart of this poem—turns our human handiwork into a meeting place of heaven and earth; God's blessing wipes away its imperfection. In our turning toward God there may be an overcoming of the separation between time and eternity, between perfection and imperfection. Our regret can cause God to regret the initial curse of Adam.

> Return, Adonai! How long will it take?
> Comfort Your servants.

God has bidden us to "return" to dust, and we too pray for a "return"—the return of God, the overcoming of our death through the timeless meeting with eternity. (The Hebrew verb used here, "comfort," is precisely the word used for the comforting of mourners, as in Isaiah's cry: Comfort ye, Comfort ye, my people.) Our return is to dust, but God's return makes of this earth a measure of Eden once again. God's return arrives when we turn. And in that moment we may meet, find comfort and a glimpse of eternity.

Perhaps it is not accidental that this poem is ascribed to "Moses, the man of God." Even Moses, "the man of God," had to face his mortality—that which he most wished for, that which was the central mission of his life, would not be achieved in his lifetime. Moses, who stands at the beginning of the biblical moment, is the primal symbol of human finitude: even Moses sinned; even Moses died; even Moses saw his life as incomplete and expressed the sense of his negligible contribution to posterity. Wholeness, completion, is not achieved by human beings. What we can accomplish is some work that has the touch of heaven, some human effort that has the mark of eternity, some act that has the blessing of God attached to it. Those moments can be lasting moments. Those deeds have the possibility of having meaning for a future generation. They have the power to enrich and sustain life. In all the book of Psalms, I know of no more poignant cry than this: establish the work of our hands—may our work, our creation, have significance too, Almighty God.

PART 3

Hope

13

Psalm 92
A Song for the Sabbath Day

HOW ELUSIVE IS THE present! As we experience it, what is occurring now can be so intensely felt that past and future seem like mere abstractions. Yet we close our eyes for a second and that which was so distinctly obvious, so immediately tangible, is gone. Heraclitus, the early Greek philosopher, famously commented that a person could never step into the same river twice, that the succession of moments made life ever-changing.

What is present passes and is then recalled in memory. From one point of view, that which occurred is now fixed; unlike that which exists now, it cannot be changed. An event happened, it had a certain outcome; someone was sick: he got well, or she died. What in the present is seen as indistinct (Will we get well? When will we die?) can now be known as fact when we think of the past. We know when we were hospitalized and when our friend died. The present may be shaky, unknown, undulating its meaning in a distant future, while the past seems securely anchored, the given of our lives. Oftentimes we turn to the past, thinking it offers a sense of fixity, that it provides a map for the present, the means by which we can assess our own contemporary story. Even though it is our own ruminations which form our memories of the past, yet it always feels like the past is a given, a finished entity, unlike the present, in which we feel vulnerable because we do not know where we are going nor can we easily predict the outcome of our actions.

Biblical Hebrew grammar seems to linguistically emphasize this perspective. Biblical Hebrew is expressive in two moments in time: actions that have been completed, a past that is fixed, given, and has a hardened, factual existence; and another reality that is open ended—what is occurring and what is yet to happen—a world that is not fixed but fluid for it is yet to come fully to be. The future tense in biblical Hebrew thus may be rightfully translated into English as a continuous present or a future, depending on context, and frequently there is a confusion as to which is the proper translation. To give just one critical example: in that seminal moment when God offers a self-revelation to Moses at the burning bush, God says, "*Ehyeh asher Ehyeh*," which has been translated both as, "I will be that which I will be," or equally, "I am that which I am." Both translations, utilizing the present or the future, have in fact had a long history. How then did the biblical reader understand this phrase, given that context doesn't indicate what the proper meaning is? Is there a correct translation? Clearly the biblical listener had a different mentality than ours, a mentality able to capture the sense of openendedness that God was conveying: tell them that there is something happening that is yet unfolding, that reality as they know it does not contain all there is. We (whose grammar expresses a more distinct sense of the present, as if it existed apart from what is soon to happen as a consequence of our acts) linguistically make an assumption of a greater order and fixity in our lives; present and future have less fluidity for us, and so we occupy a different mental ground than the biblical reader.

That difference in mentality may be said to be most critical to understanding the faith of Israel and the rhetorical stance of many psalmists. It is the future that will contain the revelation of God. The present only holds a hint of what might be; the present has yet to reveal its meaning, has to unfold its hidden purpose; otherwise it would be the past, it would be already fixed. When the situation of the psalmist is one of distress, one in which the current reality does not validate the claims of faith (for instance, that the good should prosper and evil be defeated), the psalmist can appeal to a world which is in process of becoming, the God who will fully be revealed in the future, but whose whole purpose is not disclosed in the present. Read right, i.e., with the eyes of faithfulness, the present can disclose the coming of a fuller revelation of the truth of our being, for the present is but a hint of the unfolding future.

What the faithful have to depend on is their dream, their hope, that which they anticipate—that a time will come when everyone will see the tangible worth of goodness in the same way that it is so clearly imprinted in the heart of the faithful. To the outsider, the life of faith is the world of fantasy and illusion, the claims of faith are contradicted by the toughness of contemporary realities; to the believer, the present is only an unfolding of truths which are yet to be seen in their fullness—to accept current reality as truth is to substitute the shell for the nut: a terrible mistake. What is fantasy for the one is truth and reality for the other.

Biblical prophets were so overcome by the reality of their faith that they frequently describe future hope in the past tense, as if it had already been accomplished. Prophetic poetry sees God's expected, but unaccomplished, acts so vividly that the past tense is used to describe an activity of God that is yet to be performed. The prophets thus experience God's promise as already accomplished, so certain are they of God's fidelity to the divine word. Future possibility has become fact—the future is not openended but already determined. The psychological translation of wish or faith into reality generates this grammatical jump.

So the modern reader of the Bible is confronted with descriptions of the past that are really about the future, and with a future tense that may describe the present. Translating all of this into contemporary language is a daunting task. Most frequently, any translation will have to hide the ambiguity of the Hebrew. That is the cost of translation—a language's peculiarity, its delicious resonances and overtones and so its ambiguities, have to be sacrificed to achieve meaning in a foreign tongue.

Additionally, psalms, like all poetry, are replete with intended verbal confusion. God is described by the psalmist as having helped the devotee, when in fact, we learn through the course of the psalm that God's aid is what the psalmist prays for—help is yet to come. Thus, on reading a psalm through, we may come to the end and realize how time has been manipulated and how expectation and hope have been depicted as a visible reality. Eventually, we come to understand that faith creates its own truth, and that if we let the words carry us on their wings, then the strength of the psalmist's belief provides us, as readers, with hope as well.

Psalm 92 is built out of a deliberate confusion of past, present, and future. One may read through the Hebrew several times before recognizing which parts of the psalm are talking about the past, which about the future, and which about the present. The opening attribution of the psalm is "A song for the Sabbath day," and the confusion of tenses may be one of the reasons the tradition selected this as the Sabbath psalm, for in Jewish tradition the Sabbath is simultaneously a commemoration of beginnings—the two versions of the Ten Commandments relate it to creation, on the one hand, and the exodus from Egypt on the other—and it is also traditionally understood as a foretaste of the sublime future that will be our portion at the end of time: the completion of the work of creation which is our ongoing present. And finally, in its simplest meaning, the Sabbath is the ending of the ordinary, current workweek and experienced as present time. Later Jewish Sabbath ritual observance combines all these elements, and described Friday night as a celebration of creation, the Sabbath day as a celebration of Sinai and Torah, and Saturday afternoon as a messianic moment.

PSALM 92

1   *A Psalm. A song for the Sabbath day.*

2   It is good to thank God,
       and sing to Your name, Most High:

3   to proclaim Your kindly love at daybreak,
       Your faithfulness each night

4   with a zither and harp,
       with the sound of the lyre.

5   Because You gladdened me with Your deeds, Adonai,
       of your handiwork I chant.

6   How wonderful Your works, Adonai,
       how subtle Your designs!

7   A crude person does not know,
       the fool does not understand this:

8   that the wicked sprout like grass,
       and every evildoer blossoms,
       only to be destroyed forever.

9   But You are exalted for all time, Adonai.

10   For, Your enemies, Adonai,
       for Your enemies perish;
       all evildoers will be scattered.

11   You raise my horn high like that of a wild animal;
       I am soaked in freshening oil.

12   As my eyes peer ahead
       while my enemies rise up against me,
       my ears hear:

13   "The righteous bloom like a date palm;
       they thrive like a cedar in Lebanon;

14   planted in the house of Adonai,
       they flourish in the courts of our God.

15   In old age they still produce fruit;
       they are full of sap and freshness,"

16   proclaiming that Adonai, is upright,
       my rock, in whom there is no fault.

Let us begin our consideration of the psalm with this question of tenses that we have been exploring. The indeterminacy of Hebrew tenses can be shown in the way four different translations handle verses 11–13, a critical turning point in the psalm, pointing to its meaning:

King James Version:

11. But my horn shalt thou exalt like the horn of an unicorn:
I shall be anointed with fresh oil.
12. Mine eye also shall see my desire on mine enemies, and mine ears shall hear my desire of the wicked that rise up against me.
13. The righteous shall flourish like a palm tree . . .

The New English Bible:

11. You lift my head high, like a wild ox tossing its horn;
I am anointed richly with oil.
12. I gloat over all who speak ill of me,
I listen for the downfall of my cruel foes.
13. The righteous flourish like a palm tree . . .

Anchor Bible:

11. But you exalted my horn as if I were a wild ox,
I have been anointed with fresh oil.
12. My eyes have seen the rout of my defamers, of my evil assailants.
My ears have heard:
13. "The just will flourish like a palm tree . . .

The New Jewish Publication Society Translation:

11. You raise my horn high like that of a wild ox;
I am soaked in freshening oil.
12. I shall see the defeat of my watchful foes,
hear of the downfall of the wicked who beset me.
13. The righteous bloom like a date-palm . . .

The King James Version places the whole force of these verses in the future: the poet currently resides amid a world in which good and evil are intermixed, the future holds out the promise of triumph. The Anchor Bible translation sees all that has occurred as having taken place in the past: this is a psalm of thanksgiving; the enemy has been defeated, good has triumphed, and now the devotee celebrates. The New English Bible translates the entire passage in the present, though in the end there is a hint that we may be talking of the future—if one listens for the downfall of one's enemies, then they have not yet been defeated. The sense of presentness moving toward future hope is hinted at further in the New Jewish Publication Society Translation. At first, in verse 11, the present tense is used, but in the next verse the verbs switch to the future, and then, in the end (verse 13), this translation is in the present tense but can be understood to refer to a future promise. Obviously the different readings yield quite different nuanced meanings, but all are legitimate interpretations of the possibilities created by Hebrew grammar.

I think it is not accidental that the opening and closing verbs of this psalm are infinitives: "To thank . . . to sing . . . to proclaim." Infinitives are timeless, and the confusion of the translators may represent a deliberate poetic attempt to confuse our sense of time and so touch on eternity. Perhaps just as the prophets used the past tense to describe future events, thus poetically indicating the degree of their faith in the surety of their message, so the psalmist similarly expresses an "eternal" thanksgiving through the confusion of tenses: God has helped, God is helping, God will help. At times that help is unseen; in the future it will be more obvious. Future hope unveils the constancy of God in the past and present. The poet's achievement is in making that hope so verbally convincing that it is experienced as present and assured. The poet lives in a timeless reality of infinitives.

Just as the psalm moves toward a description of an Edenic ending, a final triumph with a vision of the marvelous fecundity and permanence of the righteous, so it begins with a vision of creation and paradisiacal beginnings. The psalmist begins with a moment of thanksgiving, a moment when the devotee feels blessing—when there is a feeling of peace, of fullness, of song. It is a moment when the music of the spheres resonates in the music of the harp accompanying the psalmist.

Verses 5 and 6 celebrate the wonder of creation—its hidden power and meaning unfolding through the course of time.

> Because You gladdened me with Your deeds, Adonai,
> of your handiwork I chant.
>
> How wonderful Your works, Adonai,
> how subtle Your designs!

While the psalmist begins by alluding to God's current help in difficult circumstances, there is a more significant reference to creation itself. "How wonderful are your works . . . how subtle Your designs," surely implies principles inherent in the universe (the beauty that we see each day, the wonder we can remark on), these the poet understands to be the consequence of God's hand in creation. For a moment, the initial paradisiacal time of the inception of the universe is evoked, when God's intent and God's creation were one, and all was as wonderful as it should be. In the beginning, God's presence was obvious, altogether known—and looking at the nighttime sky or the break of dawn, we can once again experience the wonder of creation.

Then verse 7 introduces the first negative note in the psalm:

> A crude person does not know,
> the fool does not understand this:

What the psalmist sees as inherent in creation is not visible to everyone; a large segment of humanity does not see it. What was obvious at the onset of time is now a hidden process at work in the universe. The goodness of creation, the triumph of God, is not clear. In fact, the classic question of theodicy disturbs the picture of a beneficent universe: in the present, the good do not win out, but are beaten down; it appears to us as if evil can triumph as easily as—or worse, more easily than—the good. God's presence can be facilely disregarded by those who look at the surface of the world, events as they are. But time will tell a different story:

> that the wicked sprout like grass,
> and every evildoer blossoms,
> only to be destroyed forever.
>
> But You are exalted for all time, Adonai.

Those who don't trust in God look at a world in which justice does not prevail, and these assume that that's all there is. They feel that no other forces operate in the universe save their own power. They see the blossoming of materialism and selfishness and they join in what they think is the joyous life. They don't understand that there is a promised future quite different from present reality.

Now we begin to understand the importance of time in this poem. The religious axis rests on future promise that will overcome the present. The nature of faith is that it makes a claim to a reality not yet visible, but the promise of the future is so real that for the believer it is already here. Faith in the goodness of creation insists on understanding truth and justice to be the organizing principle of the universe, inherent in creation. Those who have power and use it corruptly assume that current conditions, ones in which evil seems untrammeled by consequences, will continue triumphantly. But how fleeting is their triumph from the perspective of the divine.

This psalm then, confronts the central problem of Jewish theology, the fact that the experienced and visible world does not reflect the promise of creation, and therefore tests the claim that God rules a moral universe. The pious can but appeal to the future in which contemporary contradictions will be resolved.

> For, Your enemies, Adonai,
> for Your enemies perish;
> all evildoers will be scattered.

There will come a time of clarity when goodness will reign, and it is this vision of a future world order that gives the psalmist strength to live in the present with religious faithfulness. Whatever noise there is in the world, whatever shouts of triumph are now declaimed by those in power, the psalmist's inner ear hears something else. In fact, this future calling is the overwhelming sound that the faithful hear in the here and now. This calling is so sure that the rest of the poem is a confusion of tenses—past, present and future giving rise to the alternative translations we presented in the opening of our comments.

> You raise my horn high like that of a wild animal;
> I am soaked in freshening oil.

The faithful poet now describes a dream, a vision. The righteous will be bathed in oil, as is a hero. The horn of victory will be raised.

And more. The righteous will be planted in God's house. The vision of God, the closeness to God, so yearned for, will be forever theirs. Until now the scene of the poem has been the world. Now it is the Temple, or perhaps an idealized temple. It is as if the world has been transformed into the temple, or more precisely, the life of the righteous is conducted in God's temple. We may be in exile, we may be journeying through the world, we are certainly east of Eden, but faith places us in God's house. And the righteous will be the welcoming pillars planted firmly at the entrance to God's house. According to the rabbis, outside the temple were two pillars of unequal size. Archaeologists have found such stele at the entrance of temples dating from biblical times unearthed in the land of Israel. The righteous will be such pillars, but not dead stone, they will be living, blossoming trees.

The cedar and the palm tree are interesting images. Cedars grow on the highest mountains of the Middle East, in Lebanon; palm trees flourish in the lowest area on earth—in the Jordan Valley rift. Cedars spread wide and are among the oldest living trees on earth; date palms characteristically grow new leaves annually, which spread out on the top of the trunk only; the old leaves dry up and fall away. Palms yield fruit. In ancient times dates were one of the most significant sources of energy in the human diet, but the trunk of the date palm, its wood, is practically useless. On the other hand, cedars yield no fruit, but the trunks provide beautiful hardwood, precious for building, and so the Bible records that Solomon's temple was built of Lebanon's cedarwood. In God's house, the individual diversity of the entire human species will be blessed, will be counted, will have a front row view of God. The cedar and the palm, seemingly so distant and distinct from one another, will be planted together, each saluting at the entrance to God's house,[1]

> proclaiming that Adonai is upright,
> my rock, in whom there is no fault.

The poem began by announcing how good it is to proclaim God's faithful love; the poet next imagines God singing in her own inner ear; now, at the end, she returns to her own final proclamation.

And here we have returned to the world of infinitives with which the poem began—the Hebrew reads, "to proclaim." It might well be translated "will proclaim . . ." or "Proclaiming . . ."—future or present? Does the line refer to that future moment just alluded to, or does it refer back to the beginning, to the contemporary psalmic recitation? Has the poet received enough assurance so that she is now able to announce God's righteousness, or will this song only be sung when God's righteousness is manifest in the end of time?

I believe the poet has deliberately finessed the question, and in doing so tells us a great deal about the way we should understand many psalms and the purpose of their recitation. The intonation of the psalm is both an announcement about future hope and also the creation of that future moment in the present. Through the statement of belief the devotee places herself within the purified precincts of the temple and experiences the closeness to God that the proper ritual action in the temple provides. The recitation itself constitutes the foretaste of the future reality. It is the proclamation

---

1. My friend Joe Reimer shared this insight with me.

that causes one to be planted in God's house, and it is the planting in God's house that allows one "to proclaim." The devotee reciting the poem, in fact, experiences the presence of God in the here and now through the very act of speaking of this hope. The enunciation of the poem is itself the act of deliverance. It is the singing and the telling that opens us to another reality. Past, present, and future are conflated in this moment of recitation. Hope, future wish, is made present reality through verbal imagining.

It is perhaps in this sense that the psalmist remarks that the fault is not in God; God's presence can be experienced even now by the devotee, even in this world, which certainly does have its faults and difficulties. But the universe contains a transcendent and eternal message of the presence of God captured by the song of the poet.

"In the end is our beginning," and in the beginning intimations of "the end."[2] The poem has turned back on itself:

> It is good to thank God,
> and sing to Your name, Most High:
>
> to proclaim Your kind love at daybreak,
> Your faithfulness each night
>
> with a zither and harp,
> with the sound of the lyre.

The telling and singing goes on, eternally, in God's house, here and now, before and beyond. It is the telling, the recitation, that allows us to enter into the eternal moment. It is the singing of the psalm that plants us as pillars in the entranceway of God's house.

And the tradition tied this psalm to the Sabbath, the day on which we can stop the work of the week and sing to God. Entering the Sabbath and reciting this psalm we are allowed a poetic moment in which eternity is made present—if we are faithful, if we recite the celebratory words.[3]

---

2. *The Four Quartets*, in Eliot, *The Complete Poems and Plays*.

3. Until the creation of the service welcoming the Sabbath by the sixteenth-century Jewish mystics of Safed, the recitation of Psalm 92 constituted the opening liturgy of the eve of the Sabbath in many places.

14

Psalm 150
Celebration

AND SO WE COME to the end. We began with Psalm 1, and in the course of analyzing the poem discussed how appropriate it was as the opening of the book and that its placement there was clearly intentional; and now we come to the end, to the final psalm, 150, and clearly here too there is intentionality in its placement. This psalm contains the most fulsome praise of God, a rising chorus of music and human voice ending with all of humanity joining in the praise.

The prophet Zechariah, describing the imagined idyllic future sums up his vision, saying, "On that day will God be one and God's name one." It is a line that is quoted at the conclusion of each Jewish service. God is one in the heavens, but the acknowledgment of God is hardly single-minded here on earth. We should never forget that in the Hebrew Bible the acknowledgment is not only a matter of belief, of verbal presentation, but of acts that demonstrate this belief. Thus what would constitute the acknowledgment of God would be the establishment of God's kingdom here on earth: justice would rule, peace would reign, the people Israel would be safe in their land worshiping God, each person would acknowledge the other as his or her neighbor, the stranger would be welcomed, the poor fed: "On that day, God would be King over all the earth" (Zechariah 12:9). Isaiah, the conjurer of verbal images, concludes his book with a vision of all humanity coming to God's mountain and members of each nation serving as priests in a reconstituted temple; earlier Isaiah had envisioned all creation being at peace in a future golden time: the lion and the lamb lying down together. It is a dream of a return to Eden in the fullness of time. The wish that God be coordinate with God's name on earth is a dream of the meeting of heaven and earth.

Psalm 150 captures a similar expression of the fullness of humanity, indeed of all living things coming together. The psalmist ends the book of Psalms with a unified chorus of all living beings.

PSALM 150

1 Hallelujah/Praise God
   Praise God in His sanctuary;
   praise Him in the sky, His stronghold.

2 Praise Him for His victories;
   praise Him for His exceeding greatness.

3 Praise with blasts of the horn;
   praise with harp and lyre.

4 Praise with timbrel and dance;
   praise with lute and pipe.

5 Praise with resounding cymbals;
   praise with loud-clashing cymbals.

6 Let all that breathes praise God.
   Praise God/Hallelujah

The first Hebrew word and last Hebrew word of the psalm are exactly the same—"Praise God/Hallelujah"—and frame the psalm. Each line of the poem begins with the same root word as this beginning and ending "praise" (*halleluhu*). Only once is that varied: in the second line where the verse reads "Praise God" and uses the generic name of God, *El*, rather than the shortened personal name of God used at the beginning and the end: *Yah*. (The Hebrew letter *yod* was represented by the English letter *j* instead of *y* in the King James Bible, and this identification has persisted.) The poem is a roll call of praise unfolding between opening and closing words, declaiming the praise of God.

All these repetitions, which form a rhythmic litany, are not simply reiterations. There is a crescendo of images in the psalm. The poem begins with the evocation, "Praise God in God's sanctuary," and ends with the line, "Let all that breathes praise God." The psalm commences by taking note of the praise being offered by the congregants assembled in the temple, and concludes by seeing the praise as having more universal significance: what is happening here in the temple is a reflection of the thanksgiving that all of life will express for the Creator. The psalm moves from the particular moment in the life of the assembled congregation to an enlarged sense that what the pilgrims are expressing is a reverberation of what is to happen on a universal plane. That movement from smaller to greater is evoked in the inner development of the psalm.

This simple psalm is composed of two stanzas, the first, verses 1–2, expressing praise as speech, the second, verses 3–6, describing a musical orchestra of praise. The first stanza moves from the earthly praise of God to the heavenly praise of God and finally to the evocation of the acts of God tying heaven and earth together.

> Praise God in His sanctuary;
> praise Him in the sky, His stronghold.
>
> Praise Him for His victories;
> praise Him for His exceeding greatness.

God is on earth, here with the faithful; God is in heaven, seated in majesty. God can be detected in all the wonderful acts that befall us. In this psalm of praise, heaven and earth are united; they mirror each other, there is no difference between them. God's acts bring heaven and earth together.

The second stanza opens with a blast of the horn and then moves from the soft string instruments to the rhythm section of the orchestra, finally ending with the evocation of the loudest instruments: the banging cymbals. The development is from soft sound to the loudest noise. The crescendoing orchestra is a model for the developing images of the poem. This poem is like a Russian doll in reverse. The smaller dolls inside reveal larger ones without, till the largest—"everything that has breath"—is uncovered. As we have remarked, the psalm moves from the evocation of the temple chorus to the chorus of praise of all of humanity and all living beings. Perhaps this is meant to be a reflection of the life of the faithful who initially hear God's voice as a thin diaphanous line, and then increasingly experience God's presence as overwhelming. It is an act of imagination which extends what is happening in the temple to the chorus of praise of all that lives.

Psalm 150, full of rhythmic repetition of a single root word throughout the psalm, thus contains a resounding liturgical crescendo. Words build on words so that the whole poem, made up of simple repetitive elements, is greater than its parts. The building imagery makes my own voice sound louder to me for having voiced the psalm. I, the single person reciting these words, am part of a larger chorus of creation who have experienced God's presence. Stravinsky, in setting this psalm to music in his beautiful *Symphony of the Psalms*, eschewed the obvious scoring of each line to the appropriate instrument in the orchestra. Instead, though each instrument is evoked by the words, the music marches on, emphasizing the rhythm. In this way, Stravinsky interprets what I think is inherent in the psalm: the words are not necessarily directions to the temple orchestra but are an imaginative evocation of a sacred orchestra. We live with the words, the music is yet to come. We praise God in the temple, but true blessing is to be prayed for. God's name is evoked by us, the worshipers, but the reality of the godly kingdom on earth is yet to be. Our singing, though, our voicing these words, our giving our imagination iteration, has the power to evoke that end time, to bring it into being in this moment of heartfelt outpouring. Our chorus of praise can sound as if it fills the whole world. The speaking of the words, in a heartfelt way, allows us to taste that future we hope for. For a moment, as we recite the psalm, we and the congregants who surround us, we are caught up in the singing and the praise becomes all we hear—it fills our world.

And so it is with this orchestral symphony of praise that the book of Psalms ends. The book began with the single individual, one person who is righteous, and ends with all that has God's breath praising God. The book begins with the righteous person studying God's word at home, at night, and ends with everyone present in the temple singing together. At its best, the book has offered us words that connect us in our common humanity. Its recitation allows us to enter into a deeper reality than we may have known before. The book may have helped us to face our emptiness and find our way back to a world of blessing and thanksgiving.

The voices contained in the book of Psalms can be strikingly different and the means through which they offer comfort to the reader can be quite varied. Some psalmists encourage us to look to the future for hope: not to be discouraged by what we see around us now but to look toward a promised time. For some, that promised time is close at hand; for others, it unfolds in God's counting, but for both it is a time when justice will reign, goodness be repaid, God's presence clearly felt, the light promised for the righteous made visible.

Still other psalmists offer the possibility of experiencing God's hand even now—if not visibly in the triumph of God's kingship, then at least in the life of the heart, in the deepest parts of our consciousness. And still others seek to strengthen our courage through the force of rhetoric and the power of metaphor. It is as if poetic art itself, the inspired use of language and imagination, will be sufficient to save us.

Similarly, it is striking to note how many different voices we hear in psalms: some lines impress us as quotations of then-current religious formulas; other verses feel as if they were pieties spoken by priests or elders. In many, we can clearly hear the voice of supplicants, simple men and women looking to God for help: people, pilgrims perhaps, pouring out their hearts with complaints, pleas, prayers of thanksgiving, expressions of regret, diary pages of their inner lives. Sometimes among the voices we hear is God's own: the psalmist imagines God's response to our plea and so offers what is the ultimate hoped-for comfort. For many through the generations, this is what they heard as they read the psalms—God's voice speaking to them—mediated perhaps through godly people, divine instruments, but certainly offering a whispered response to their own pain.

Some of us may feel that too as we read psalms; for others, what psalms offer is at least this: voices enunciating the same concern our own souls contain. Here are poems that give expression to the most deeply felt spiritual moments—joy, despair, hope. The words of the psalmists, so deeply felt, so artfully displayed, frequently so simple, most often profoundly expressed, can become an accompaniment to our own spiritual journey. In reading these words we are comforted, if only for having found a voice to join with our own.

Sometimes in my own loneliness, I too am able to join in the psalmist's chorus, and hear a voice of redemption.

Bibliography of Quoted Sources

Adar, Zvi. *The Book of Psalms*. Tel Aviv: Tcherikover, 1976. (Hebrew)

Alter, Robert. *The Book of Psalms: A Translation with Commentary*. New York: Norton, 2007.

Buber, Martin. *Good and Evil*. New York: Scribner, 1953.

Brueggemann, Walter. *The Message of the Psalms: A Theological Commentary*. Minneapolis: Augsburg, 1984.

Dahood, Mitchell. *Psalms*. Anchor Bible vols. 16, 17, 17a. Garden City, NY: Doubleday, 1966, 1968, 1970.

Elliot, T. S. *The Complete Poems and Plays, 1909–1950*. New York, Harcourt Brace, 1958.

Gunkel, Hermann. *The Psalms: A Form-Critical Introduction*. Translated by Thomas M. Horner. Facet Books: Biblical Series 19. Philadelphia: Fortress, 1967.

Levine, Herbert. *Sing unto God a New Song: A Contemporary Reading of the Psalms*. Indiana Studies in Biblical Literature. Bloomington: Indiana University Press, 1995.

Sarna, Nahum M. *On the Book of Psalms: Exploring the Prayers of Ancient Israel*. New York: Schocken, 1993.

Simon, Uriel. *Four Approaches to the Book of Psalms: From Saadiah Gaon to Abraham Ibn Ezra*. Translated by Lenn J. Schramm. SUNY Series in Judaica. Albany: State University of New York Press, 1991.

Wieder, Laurance, editor. *The Poets' Book of Psalms: The Complete Psalter as Rendered by Twenty-Five Poets from the Sixteenth to the Twentieth Centuries*. San Francisco: HarperSanFrancisco, 1995.

Psalms Translations Consulted

The Holy Bible containing the Old and New Testaments. New York: American Bible Society.

JPS Tanakh. 2nd ed. Philadelphia: Jewish Publication Society, 1999.

Levi, Peter. *The Psalms*. New York: Penguin, 1976.

The New English Bible with the Apocrypha. New York: Oxford University Press, 1971.

The Psalms: A New Translation from the Hebrew Arranged for Singing from the Psalmody of Joseph Gelineau. Deus Books. New York: Paulist, 1968.